The Executive Guide to Enterprise Risk Management

This page is intentionally left blank

The Executive Guide to Enterprise Risk Management

Christopher Chappell

First published 2014 by
PALGRAVE MACMILLAN

Palgrave Macmillan in the UK is an imprint of Macmillan Publishers Limited, registered in England, company number 785998, of Houndmills, Basingstoke, Hampshire RG21 6XS.

Palgrave Macmillan in the US is a division of St Martin's Press LLC, 175 Fifth Avenue, New York, NY 10010.

Palgrave Macmillan is the global academic imprint of the above companies and has companies and representatives throughout the world.

Palgrave® and Macmillan® are registered trademarks in the United States, the United Kingdom, Europe and other countries

ISBN 978-1-349-47696-1   ISBN 978-1-137-37454-7 (eBook)
DOI 10.1057/9781137374547

This book is printed on paper suitable for recycling and made from fully managed and sustained forest sources. Logging, pulping and manufacturing processes are expected to conform to the environmental regulations of the country of origin.

A catalogue record for this book is available from the British Library.

A catalog record for this book is available from the Library of Congress.

For Cenan, Jemima and Zachary
With love

Contents

List of Figures

List of Tables

Preface

In writing this book, I am by no means claiming to have invented or discovered all the concepts and frameworks presented here. In various guises, many of them have been common theories for a number of years, and I have been influenced by them in my day-to-day work.

This book was written to provide a practical guide to assist senior executives in understanding, challenging and using the tools within enterprise risk management in a way that enhances the value created from the management of the business.

As the captain of a rowing club, I had many people come to me wanting always to use the best and most expensive boats in the boathouse. They believed their ability to win was hindered by the quality of the equipment they were required to use. This was rarely the case. There is little point in having the finest equipment and materials if you do not know how to use them. In fact, rowing in a boat that has been designed for more significantly experienced rowers can hinder performance more than enhance it.

The same is true here. The amount of recent regulatory change has meant material amounts of money have been spent on evolving the way companies operate, in some cases investing in state-of-the-art equipment. However, if we cannot bring all these pieces together in a way to enhance insight into the business, we have a very big white elephant to maintain.

Hence, the book.

1
Introduction

For years, the desire for enterprise risk management (ERM) frameworks has been driven by regulatory demands and companies seeking stronger credit ratings to ensure that capital can be raised more cheaply. Acquiring a budget for such developments is easiest when driven by a regulatory demand. However, this can make it more difficult to achieve buy-in and a belief in the benefits of such a framework when attempting to embed it in the business. Simplistically, the value to the business is achieved by answering the question 'What's in it for me?'

For most companies, the challenge remains as to how to stop ERM frameworks from becoming white elephants.

Publications outline the major benefits of an ERM framework, including improved business performance resulting from a clearer view of which activities add value, and greater transparency around the rationale for making the decision to take on certain risks. Why is this different from the past?

For a period up to the 1990s, some companies had used accounting techniques to control the volatility of their earnings. Management relied on the 'good times' (times of making premium returns on risks) to provide the return to restore the margins held to manage future fluctuations. In the current business environment, these practices are no longer acceptable. Economically, this is not sustainable in the longer term as it suggests risks are not being understood properly or managed. ERM helps management understand its risks and provides a framework to ensure they can be managed or mitigated. The old adage of 'know your business' is now more true than ever – at its core, knowing your business is about knowing what the risks are, why you are taking them and how they are mitigated.

The vision for ERM is that it enables the business to grow shareholder value through making smart risk-return-based decisions.

This means

- optimising the risk-return opportunities, allocating capital appropriately to support initiatives that grow the business and identify, reduce or balance the amount of capital-backing areas from which insufficient benefit is being achieved;
- developing a charge for products and services in a way that reflects the risks being taken;
- being able to ask the questions that should be asked to understand the uncertainties that exist within opportunities, such that the Board can make fully informed and balanced decisions – a 'no surprises' culture.

Running a successful business is about pursuing the right business strategy based on the opportunities that exist given the company's financial and managerial capabilities. ERM ensures the business has the right information, available at the right time to identify and assess opportunities and make decisions with an explicit understanding of the key issues.

In turn, this gives rise to increased organisational effectiveness as a result of the business having the right information available to make decisions such that opportunities can be entered and exited in a timely manner to optimise the return. This capability will enhance the company's reputation across many stakeholders, including regulators and rating agencies, by evidencing the executive is skilled enough to manage the uncertainties, demonstrably reducing the likelihood of insolvency directly or indirectly. This is what leads to improved access to capital markets over the long term, with reduced costs of financing, as it is clear that you 'know your business'.

This book examines four questions to be addressed when seeking to create a successful ERM framework:

1. How can I utilise the risk management tools to help me optimise my strategy?
2. How does risk appetite help me meet my performance objectives and help me assess risk-return optimisation and allocate capital efficiently and effectively?
3. How can I challenge the experts to test whether my information is robust?
4. How do I develop a culture that will support the traits of people in great companies – courage, humility, self-control and passion?

2
Defining Enterprise Risk Management

This chapter seeks to define risk and enterprise risk management (ERM). In particular, it will provide an executive's view of the purpose of an ERM framework.

Since the inception of ERM, a lot of time, effort and financial resources have been dedicated to the enhancement of companies' ability to manage risk. Within the phrase 'enterprise risk management', the use of the term 'risk' is now rather misleading as it has evolved over the same period from a word that related to the ability to apply internal controls to a word used to cover how a business is managed strategically. This has led to a lot of confusion and debate about what ERM is and how it interacts with other aspects of managing a business.

The term 'risk' is more usefully articulated as the 'uncertainty of outcome, good or bad'.

Some observers define risk as the quantifiable element, and 'uncertainty' as the non-quantifiable dimension. However, we find this difficult as all aspects of what we do involve making some form of judgment about the implications of events based on available information. Not all that information is directly relevant, and those judgments themselves may not be borne out in practice. Hence, the line between risk and uncertainty being quantifiable and non-quantifiable may only exist in the minds of those who live in the mathematical 'modelled world', rather than those who operate in the 'real world'.

The following framing of ERM may add to the growing list of definitions:

Enterprise risk management is a framework that supports the way in which a company runs its business, and that defines its approach to assessing and managing the uncertainty of the outcome of its plan consistently with how it manages its capital and value creation activities.

An alternate approach to defining ERM is through the eyes of a chief executive officer (CEO) as he or she meets the Board to position the strategy and how it will be delivered:

'As CEO, I am aiming to deliver the business plan, which encapsulates our vision for the organisation over the coming years. I want to make sure the plan is delivered in a manner that is within the boundaries we established as "our way of getting things done around here", and that manages the dynamic tensions between the various stakeholder groups.

The plan outlines the uncertainties and volatility that we face over the planning horizon, the sorts of issues that might emerge to prevent us from achieving the plan, and what we believe we can do to keep things on track should these arise.

As an executive team, we are fully aware that events may occur that give rise to new opportunities, and we have a framework that helps us, on an ongoing basis, identify these opportunities, determine the implications of taking them and understand how we can go about harnessing them.

As the plan is broken down into bite-sized segments, such as the budget and forecast for the coming year, I have outlined how we make sure that information of sufficient quality is delivered in a timely manner in order for us to assess what is happening and whether we need to take action in full knowledge of all the relevant facts. This includes the systems and tools that underpin getting the right information to the decision-makers at the right time and in a way that can help them make those decisions.

To make this process operate efficiently and effectively, my management team needs to have the appropriately delegated authority to take action on a day-to-day basis so that they can manage the delivery of their components of the plan. To avoid confusion and angst about what we do within the business, the Board needs to clarify where the authority that has been delegated starts and ends, to ensure that when an event occurs that is significant, others have been engaged appropriately, or if it is sufficiently material, the Board has been engaged.

In order to ensure that the Board feels comfortable delegating this authority to the executive team, we have ensured that the executive team

– has an appropriate skill set and expertise to deliver their responsibilities within these delegated authorities,

– knows how to behave appropriately when faced with decisions or the need to communicate information, and

– are remunerated in a way that encourages the right sort of behaviour and actions.

Having agreed upon this framework, we will cascade this down and through the organisation in a consistent manner, communicating the link between the strategy and employees' operational limits and performance objectives so that people are not working in silos and know how what they do impacts the delivery of the plan for the whole organisation'.

This is a top-down view of ERM, which concerns how a company goes about doing things. The advantage of adopting this approach is that it highlights the key value-adding areas, which is useful when trying to build a business case for a Board to assist them to understand what benefit they will obtain for the investment in time and money.

It is also essential to separate ERM from the historic role of risk functions, as it is now evolving to include more about seeing risk management as the identification of strategic opportunities rather than purely a process for monitoring internal controls.

The driver for evolution is that people invest in companies for them to take risks in order to earn a return. Where there is risk, there is opportunity

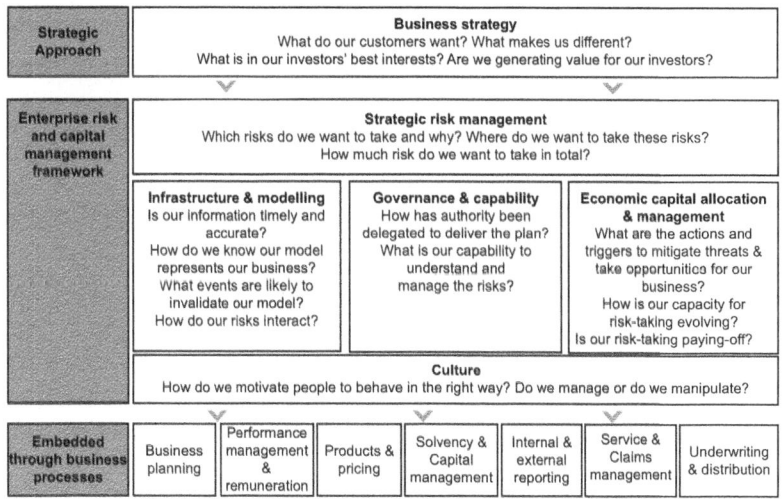

Figure 2.1 A business operating model

to make a return – the decision is whether that is a risk-return trade-off that the company wants to take.

Figure 2.1 outlines the holistic ERM framework, shaping and informing the business strategy and operating through the key processes that deliver the results throughout the year – effectively the Business Operating Model. Additionally, if one can imagine the information flows between these components, it is possible to develop a report that includes these aspects, which under Solvency 2, the new European regulatory framework, would be known as an Own Risk and Solvency Assessment.

The ERM framework in Figure 2.1 illustrates how risk management is integral to the development of the strategic plan and facilitates an understanding of which risks are producing an optimal profile of returns and how capital can be allocated effectively to make this happen. Achieving this is as much about the capabilities to understand the risks we choose to take and the reasons why we did not take others.

The ERM framework illustrates how decision-making needs to be supported by the infrastructure and models capable of delivering accurate information in a timely manner, with management in full knowledge of the shortcomings of the models so that they can apply their judgment effectively.

The delegation of authority exists to help us respond operationally to day-to-day fluctuations and issues efficiently and effectively, escalating for approval when events and situations are more extreme.

Those to whom authority has been delegated need to act as behavioural role models, as others will be watching them for clues to the appropriate way to react, respond and manage issues when they arise.

3
Developing a Business Strategy

This chapter provides coverage of the various dimensions of a business strategy (i.e. the profit strategy, the risk strategy and the capital strategy) and how executives can question proposals to gain insight into the challenges facing its delivery. In particular, it will outline:

– how to shape a profit strategy,
– how to develop a risk strategy,
– the purpose of a capital strategy,
– the difference between solvency and capital management.

The purpose of a business strategy

The key question is: what is the difference between business planning and business strategy?

The core to a business strategy is developing the 'competitive advantage' or determining 'what makes us different from others'. Without the threat from competition, there would be little need for a strategy, as the company could just plan how it would continue over the coming years without any need to differentiate itself. Thus, the focus of developing any form of strategy is to understand how a company can gain a sustainable difference from its competitors in an efficient manner. The plan highlights how the strategy will be delivered.

There is a lot of talk about 'lean' and 'six sigma' continuous improvement processes, product profitability improvement plans, and tracking and responding to competitors' price changes as a part of the strategy. However, these actions relate to improving the company's financial capability or maintaining a market position rather than creating a sustainable competitive difference. Customers will tolerate a certain price differential for the benefit of what you offer that's different, as long as that price difference is not too great. Hence, not taking these actions, and being suboptimal in some way, will be tolerated for a while, but not to the point where the price differential becomes too great. Hence, these activities are not sources of a sustainable competitive difference.

Strategy is about understanding and positioning the company relative to its competitors. Managing strategy is about maintaining and enhancing that relative position.

The business model

One of the key inputs to the development of the strategy is an understanding of the business model of the organisation. The business model outlines what the business does and how it makes money in doing it. This assists stakeholders, both internally and externally, in understanding where the return is expected to come from and the sort of risks the business is expected to take to achieve it.

Sustainable profitability = profit from industry ± profit from differentiation

$$\pi \qquad = \qquad \beta \qquad \pm \qquad \alpha$$

In market terms, the performance of the market is deemed as β (beta). We are looking for what gives us the α (alpha). The profit from differentiating, α, could equally be a negative as a positive outcome. The negative outcome may arise when the organisation delivers a benefit that is less than the additional cost as part of its positioning, with the benefit viewed as more important than the enhanced return. This differentiator might come about through taking an ethical position that causes a drag on overall return but is important to those whom the business serves, or through a service level and approach that are desired by a segment of the market, which means the same return is not achieved. In essence, financial outperformance need not be the only driver of a competitive difference.

Articulating the source of differentiation is the starting point. A key output of the strategy is understanding how to bring about the conditions that most favour this desired strategic position relative to that of competitors, and an ability to determine realistic responses for when to enter and exit opportunities to build that position, or when to accept a compromise as markets change. This desired outcome aligns well with what we want from our enterprise risk management (ERM) framework.

It should be accepted that any proposed solution to delivering a business strategy is not going to be the perfect business plan, as the perfect solution does not exist. The proposal needs to be one that will enable the organisation to improve its position relative to that of its competitors at an acceptable cost.

Developing the strategic position and the source of competitive advantage

To develop this distinctive strategic position, an organisation needs to consider a number of basic questions:

1. *What is the proposition?*
   The proposition is about the benefits or space that the company will deliver that is different from that of its competitors. It is what the company could be best at[1], and what it is passionate about.

2. *What is the measure of success?*
   To produce a sustainable long-term business, the measure of success needs to align in some way with the creation of genuine economic value. Simply put, the company needs to provide products or services for the customer at a price that exceeds the cost of providing it.

3. *What it is the company foregoing to be different?*
   As a result of choosing a particular way of being different, a company is likely to opt to forego some opportunities. It is important to understand explicitly what these are and why, just as it is equally important to understand what the strategy is not as well as what it is. This can help stakeholders understand the decisions that are made and provide the basis for a continuity of direction that enables the company to focus on developing the key skills to support the delivery of the difference and building a good reputation and brand in the marketplace.

4. *Which processes within the company create value?*
   A company consists of a series of processes and operations that result in the provision of a number of services or products to a market. All these processes must operate in a way that supports all other processes. For example, the design of a product should support the company's approach to distribution, and both should integrate with the way in which the company plans to deliver its post-sales service. Without understanding how the activities fit together, it is difficult for the company to ensure that the strategy and the whole system of operation

mutually reinforce. It is also important to understand which parts of these processes add value and thus, which parts of these processes the company wishes to provide through in-house or outsourced arrangements. Some of the considerations of 'value' in this assessment are the contribution to profit that are made from each aspect of the process; the amount of capital that is put at risk; and the people, skills and systems required to deliver the process. For example, changing the approach to outsourcing a particular process will include changing the skill set required, as managing an outsourced provider will require different skills from providing a service in-house.

If a company is to differentiate itself from its competitors, it is important for it to assess how it is creating value in each of these steps and how these differ from the approach taken by its competitors. Purely adopting current best practice will result in an organisation performing most activities in a way similar to its competitors rather than doing something to gain a long-term advantage. Process improvements, even if they are the new best way of doing things, can be replicated and mimicked by competitors, and hence why they do not lead to a source of differentiation.

Within the financial services field, companies have taken different approaches to outsourcing the provision of services depending on their own circumstances. HSBC creates value in distribution and has established links with companies such as Aviva for product manufacturing; Phoenix has outsourced its investment back office support, but retained its front office in-house capabilities; LV= has outsourced its investment management; and Friends Life has outsourced its Heritage policy administration.

3.1 Components of the business strategy

Central to the operation of a company is the strategic planning process. This process provides the aggregation of the various areas of the organisation into

- a strategy for competitive differentiation,
- a set of objectives to provide a measure of success in delivering that strategy,
- a plan for delivering these objectives, and
- a framework for delegating authority from the Board to the executive team to enable that plan to be delivered efficiently and effectively on a day-to-day basis.

The business strategy is made up of the profit strategy, the risk strategy and the capital strategy.

The profit strategy describes how the economic value of the organisation (enterprise value) will be optimised, from which a plan can be developed to cover aspects such as product developments and acquisitions.

The risk strategy sets out how the organisation's attitude towards taking on various types of risk supports the organisation's efforts to position itself for competitive differentiation. This will include details of the threats and opportunities to the business strategy, and an explicit understanding of the implications of the opportunities that the organisation accepts it will forego to create its strategic position.

The capital strategy describes the approach to the capital structure and the securing of the funding required to deliver the plans (that is, debt/equity levels, how and where the capital is held, and how solvency is managed).

All aspects of the strategy link together in that:

- in order to make profits (create economic value), an organisation needs to take risks;
- in order to take risks, an organisation needs to be able to put something 'at risk', which is generally its capital and its reputation;
- in order to build the profile of risks that are going to make the organisation profits, an organisation needs capital to invest and to have a sufficient cushion above any minimum requirement in order to withstand the day-to-day fluctuations that occur, because things rarely go exactly to plan.

3.1.1   A corporate strategy

What has been discussed previously is the essence of a business strategy, which is different from a corporate strategy. Irrespective of the type of corporation[2] or Group, at the basic level a corporation aims to use capital to earn return from a diverse range of opportunities that diversify the risks, or exploit synergies such as those resulting from cash flows, distribution or research.

Hence, at this level, corporate strategy is generally defined solely in financial terms, such as a target return on equity, rather than some wider business purpose. The biggest issue in recent decades has been the perpetuation of financial metrics as the sole measure of performance for business strategies. Potentially, this is the reason why there have been a number of significant difficulties with organisational cultures as firms focussed on making profit only.

In the 1980s, the focus was on making as much money as you could, and thus as much profit as you could. The 2000s were marked by the drive to control expenditure, with companies aiming to operate more cost effectively for the same return and thus increase profit. In the 2010s, the focus is on trying to achieve the same return, but by taking less risk in order to make the most profit per pound of capital. Where has been the consideration of the customer?

3.2   The profit strategy

The first component of the business strategy is the profit strategy. The profit strategy identifies how the competitive differentiation will manifest itself in the market over the medium- to longer term, from which a company can develop a plan to assess how this will be delivered over the next three to five years.

3.2.1   Questions that could be asked by the Board

In finalising the profit strategy, the Board might wish to ensure that it has considered the following questions:

1. What will the market look like in five years' time?
2. What will be our role in the market in five years' time?
3. Will our competitors be the same?
4. If we need take action to change and meet the evolving position, what are the likely reactions of competitors, and what is our counteraction?
5. What do we need to do to have the capability in place to achieve our ambition?
6. Having developed a proposed growth plan, can we achieve the same return by taking an approach with less risk?
7. What would give rise to the need to change the strategy or the plan?
8. Are we clear on what assumptions have been made implicitly in finalising the strategic objectives? What needs to happen for these implicit assumptions to remain reasonable?

3.2.2   Setting the profit strategy

As a business strategy is developed with a view towards being in the right position in three to five years' time, it is important for a company to develop a strategy with this end-state in mind. The key skill is to separate yourself from the current position and assume you are operating in the desired end-state five years hence. In this position, it is important to assess what the company is doing at this point, its key new attributes and approaches, the challenges it faced on the way to achieving this, and the drivers for change within the new world in which it is operating.

What will the world look like in five years' time? This is more than just a view of the market. It is necessary to consider the changes in the political landscape and the opportunities that this might bring, as, for example, approaches to saving, healthcare and retirement might change. Your company might even be under new leadership.

The application of SWOT and PESTER analysis with a view to the company's future position can be useful in framing the considerations of its future state. For example,

- political – Who will be in government? Which issues will dominate? What is the government's attitude towards healthcare, pension or social reform? What is the government's attitude toward taxes? What legislation will the government be pushing to introduce or what legislation will have been introduced by then?
- economic – What will be the economic position of various countries? How will this impact the price of debt? How will this impact people's attitudes toward insurance and savings? How will people shop?
- social – What will be the social dynamics? What methods of social interaction will exist? How will people develop their views of companies? What social needs will exist? What will be the basis of people's buying decisions? What will prevent or deter people from buying?
- technological – What technological advances are occurring? How will customers want to do business with us? How will they impact our risk exposures? How can companies harness innovation or technology to create new rating factors for new business, and new ways of collecting premiums, paying claims, collecting evidence of claim events and managing a business?
- environmental – What impacts do changing environments have on the need for new products or the price of existing products?
- regulation – What is the impact on the attractiveness of products or the price of products from the regulations that will be in force at that time? Are there changes in the expertise required to manage the business or sell the products?

It is useful to present this analysis through an assessment for the company of the changes required to critical processes and success factors over the period. Understanding the changes required to critical processes and success factors helps identify how the relative position of competitors changes as the company evolves. The approach helps to recognize that as a market evolves, the competitor landscape may also evolve such that the competitors you once had are no longer the greatest threat. For example, process 'A' may not be critical to market success today, but it may be important in five years time. A company strong in process A may not be a direct competitor today, but would be recognized as an evolving threat in the future as you seek to enhance this critical process within your organization. The approach also helps to recognize the effort required for competitors to evolve and mimick your plans for strategic repositioning given their strengths and weaknesses today. This is a key area where risk functions can bring value.

3.2.3   Competitive differentiation

Organisations achieve competitive differentiation by providing their targeted customers with what they want better or more effectively than competitors, and in ways which their competitors find difficult to imitate.

In the future, there may be four overarching enablers for a sustainable competitive differentiation:

- Intensifying functional differentiation where this is a key factor for success. This may be through an injection of resources into a particular area to gain an advantage over competitors. Thus, while an organisation may have no more resources (or cost) than a competitor, it has created an advantage through the way it has utilised or deployed the resources within the business. For example, it may take an approach to investment management that others do not utilise.
- Identifying the critical issues and learning faster than your competitors. We are living in a world in which the pace of change is ever increasing. This means we tend to develop rational solutions for a world we recognise and understand today; however, by the time we try to implement the solution, that world has changed and the solution can appear irrational and outdated when implemented. Hence, we need to get ahead of this curve to develop appropriate 'rational' solutions for the time we don't yet live in.
- Deploying disruptive initiatives such as
  - disruptive technology to distribute the end product more effectively for the customer;
  - disruptive customers who value a different customer experience or product;
  - disruptive innovators who can create the product before the market identifies the need.

This approach may be particularly apparent in stagnating or 'well developed markets'. Consider what stopped the rot at Apple Inc in the 2000s.

– Creating a space that is not on the current 'map' and that is uniquely suited to the organisation's own strengths, and thus is difficult to imitate or to compete with.

In simple terms, you cannot be different if you just do the same thing as your competitors in the same markets.

It is not that you want to get rid of competition, but rather maintain a position that is different from it in a positive way. Competition is a good thing for any organisation. Competitors help organisations to shape their competitive difference and can help customers to benchmark the various propositions to identify why a company adds value. This benchmarking can help customers build trust in what you are doing as being reasonable and to their benefit.

Additionally, competitors can be useful in

– helping sectors absorb fluctuations in market demand that could otherwise manifest as reductions in service quality or brand damage if a company is not able to deal with the increased demand;
– servicing segments of the market you view as unattractive but that you might have been forced to serve otherwise if there were no provider.

3.3   The risk strategy

The second component of the business strategy is the risk strategy.

3.3.1   Questions that could be asked by the Board

In finalising the business strategy, the Board needs to ensure it is satisfied with the resulting risk strategy. The following provides some useful questions to be answered during this process:

1. What are the significant risks the Board is willing to accept?
2. What are the significant risks the Board is NOT willing to accept?
3. Do we understand from which risks we are expecting to make our return?
4. Is there a clear understanding of the extent of the significant risks that the organisation is proposing to take to achieve its objectives?
5. Is there a clear understanding of what could be done to bring the exposures back under control should something happen?
6. What profile of risks do we want to take in five years' time?
7. What needs to be done to evolve the risk profile from where we are to where we want to be?

8. How does the evolution of the risk profile impact the diversification benefit?
9. Do we understand the risks we are taking? Do we manage any of these risks better than our competitors?
10. Has the Board reviewed the capabilities of the organisation to manage the risks it faces and to understand how this capability will need to change in the future as the risk profile evolves?
11. Does a plan exist to ensure the capacity and expertise to manage the risks that exist at an appropriate time over the planning horizon?
12. Is there a clear articulation of the strategic objectives into limits and tolerances such that the amount of authority that has been delegated by the Board is unambiguous?
13. Does each manager understand the extent to which he or she is permitted to expose the organisation to the consequences of an event or situation?
14. Is management incentivised appropriately to manage the delivery of the plan without taking excessive risk or hiding failings?

3.3.2   Setting the risk strategy

A risk strategy is developed from the business model and helps to challenge and guide the development of the profit strategy during the business planning cycle. The ability to challenge and align the profit strategy with the risk strategy prevents the organisation from having 'nasty surprises' that it must explain to the market when losses arise from sources that were not in keeping with the business model. Furthermore, articulating a risk strategy helps an organisation in a number of ways:

– It provides a directional steer to business units when they are developing their profit plans, and a framework with which the risk function can challenge those plans. The purpose of the discussions is to ensure that the implications of adopting a strategy are understood including the key sensitivities and areas of judgment, and to ensure that the profit plan and risk strategy are aligned or, where they are misaligned, that there is an understanding and acceptance of the implication.
– It translates the high-level business strategy into operational level limits. This provides the framework within which authority can be delegated to ensure the day-to-day tasks efficiently deliver the plan.
– It optimises the use (allocation) of capital within an organisation, particularly through ensuring that the benefits resulting from risk diversification are preserved.

– It enhances the understanding and communication with external parties to bring increased credibility to what the organisation is doing and how it will earn its return without 'risking everything'.

As an integral part of the strategic considerations, the risk strategy should be reviewed in conjunction with the setting of the broader business strategy and performance measures, most usually at the start of the strategic planning process. This ensures that the strategies are aligned and that the business strategy is achievable within the constraints of the defined risk strategy and any agreed-upon limits on risk-taking activity. This alignment is critical, as a business strategy that is not achievable within the risk strategy will result in frictions within the organisation and with stakeholders on how return and risk are being managed, the strategy failing, and the risk strategy being perceived as inconsequential.

The risk strategy is not intended to be a rigid set of rules to prevent the business units from determining and executing business plans, but rather to provide guidance to the business units so as to encourage debate about the risks the organisation would prefer to take, and to ensure that the risks taken are well understood by, and appropriate to, the company as a whole.

The risk strategy tends to be articulated in a series of statements that outline the principles that underlie the organisation's proposed risk-taking. Appendix B provides a table that outlines the sort of questions that could be used to develop these risk strategy statements.

In order to structure the challenge of the profit strategy with the risk strategy, we have found the template in Table 3.1 useful. The content of Table 3.1 provides an illustrative example of how this can help close the amount of information asymmetry between a Group and a business unit when developing the strategic plan. This information is also useful in helping shape the appropriate operational limits for risk-taking and an articulation of a company's risk preferences.

3.4 The capital strategy

The third component of the business strategy is the capital strategy.

3.4.1 Questions that the Board could ask

In finalising the business strategy, the Board needs to ensure it is satisfied with the resulting capital strategy. The following provides some of the useful

Table 3.1 Example of the use of the risk strategy statement to challenge the profit strategy

Retirement business unit	Business unit Profit Strategy	Business unit view of impact of profit strategy on risk and return	Relevant challenge to alignment of profit strategy and risk strategy
Business unit profit strategy	[Simplified example provided below] Aim to acquire annuity business as we believe these provide an ability to utilise the long-term nature of insurers' balance sheets. We believe the size of the market for this business....	We have some appetite for taking longevity risk where the cost of reinsuring this risk to a third party outweighs the benefit of retaining it [expanded criteria for retaining it]. We seek illiquidity premium where this matches the term of our annuity liabilities, and recognise that this results in taking some credit risk. We generally avoid interest rate risk, as we believe the upside to be limited.	• What are the sources of risk that are being brought to the table? How does the strategy impact our other risk exposures (concentration, counterparty etc.)? Do proposed actions bring on new risks? • Are we seeking illiquidity premium in the optimal way ? Is illiquidity changing in our chosen markets? • Should credit default risk be hedged to provide 'pure illiquidity premium'? • Should we be seeking alternative asset classes to achieve illiquidity premium (e.g., infrastructure)? • What return do we expect to make from these targeted risks? What is the marginal contribution to capital requirements from these risks? How do the risk exposures impact diversification? What is the potential performance variability? Can we achieve the same return, targeting less risk? • What is our internal capability to manage the risks? If we use reinsurance, what is the level we should use, and is there a point at which the size of the portfolio should make us consider developing the in-house expertise? • Is the risk transferable/scalable? Is the pricing sufficient that we could transfer risk to a third party (i.e., can we dial the exposure up or down without compromising the risk/return?)?

- Is our portfolio of annuities sufficiently diverse such that it protects us from the risk of medical advances, for example (e.g., We acquire pension liabilities that have significant exposure to a segment of the population who are in worse than average health for whom medical advances will be more beneficial than for those of average health)?
- What does the growth trajectory of the business do to the risk profile and diversification benefit over time? Will this impact the profit plans for this business? What actions could be taken to manage any adverse risk profile development?
- What does our peer group risk profile look like?
- Does the strategy (including investment plans) have any implications for compliance, accounting, valuation or data availability?
- Can our infrastructure support the strategy, including its growth trajectory? What enhancements need to be considered?

questions to be answered during this process:

1. Do we have sufficient capital available to meet regulatory requirements in each legal entity over the next five years? What operational buffers do we need to run in each entity?
2. Where is our capital and where is our risk, and how do they move over time?
3. What structures are in place to help us move capital around the Group efficiently? What constraints do we face on capital mobility?
4. What structures exist to move our risks around the Group to where our capital resides?
5. Is the capital of sufficient liquidity to meet all the payments when they fall due?
6. What plans exist to understand how the company can react to the need to strengthen its capital position if adverse scenarios occur, or conversely, how it will utilise any excess capital?
7. What is the optimal amount and mix of capital of various types to minimise the drag on the overall return on capital? How might this change over the next five years?
8. What is the optimal cost of the capital for the purposes of use in pricing and assessing other initiatives?
9. When we put capital to work, how long is it tied up (when could we expect it back)?

3.4.2   How much capital do I need?

Companies need to hold enough capital to meet the promises they made to their customers and suppliers of services, and have a sufficient amount to invest in and grow the business without undue concern about breaching any regulatory minimum requirement as a result of the impact on their financial position of the day-to-day fluctuations in markets. The solution is not to hold as much capital as you can. There are risks to being overcapitalised, including a risk to competitiveness[3] and the ability to attract and retain investors[4]. This capital requirement for a business is known as the amount of economic capital that is required, and is one of the outputs from the development of the risk appetite outlined later.

How much capital a company holds and the risks it takes impact its return. A company aims to make a return on the capital that has been invested with it. A company can optimise its return on capital by increasing the amount of return per pound of capital, or by decreasing the amount of capital required to back the achieving of each pound of return. This is not really revolutionary thinking, but simply stated, it illustrates why understanding the risk-return profile is critically important when establishing the assessment of the types and amount of risk an organisation wants to take. We want to ensure the capital backing our risks is working efficiently and takes account of the level of volatility of return that shareholders will tolerate.

As well as understanding the amount of capital required, it is necessary to consider the mix of capital that is required (for example, debt and equity). There are a number of considerations in developing the view of the required mix of capital.

1. What financial resources are we likely to need in five years' time to optimise the cost of capital, given the uses to which the capital will be put?
2. What is the industry norm, debt/equity ratio?
3. What is the view of the credit rating agencies?
4. What initiatives do we have to invest in? What is the expected return on these investments? How much capital do we need and over what time horizon?
5. What level of losses are we willing tolerate?
6. What does our cash flow profile look like? How volatile is the likely cash flow? Have we historically delivered the cash flow plans? Will any caps on dividend payments be likely?
7. What ability do we have to service capital instruments (for example, paying debt coupons) with headroom to be able to do this as markets fluctuate?
8. What is the most efficient volume of capital to raise to optimise the cost of raising that form of capital?
9. What profile of redemption proceeds is optimal to prevent reinvestment issues from becoming critical?
10. What are the tax and regulatory implications?
11. How easily and quickly is it possible to go back to the market to raise more?
12. In what currency are our liabilities and what do we need to match?

In determining the overall capital requirement, the organisation needs to consider how this will be met from the various forms of funding (e.g. debt and equity). These types of capital funding have different abilities to absorb losses should they arise[5] and different obligations with respect to repayment.

In assessing our needs for each type of capital funding, we consider using the types of capital that are good at absorbing losses where we are willing to accept a certain size of potential loss, such as for projects that require financial backing to initiate that may result in loss of the amount invested if things go wrong. We consider using other forms of capital funding where capital is required to be held for security, and do not expect that the capital will be called upon to absorb losses, or where a series of known cash flows can be monetised to meet a more immediate liquidity demand. These considerations are targeted at being able to optimise the cost of capital because different ways of funding capital result in the investor's taking different levels of risk and therefore demanding different levels of compensation. Thus, if we do not think we need capital in order to take a certain level of risk, it is better not to pay the price for having it on the balance sheet[6].

3.4.3   What is the difference between solvency, capital and investment management?

Developing a capital strategy causes considerable confusion, the root of which, we believe, has to do with understanding the difference between the movement of capital to meet regulatory solvency requirements, the allocation of capital to particular businesses because of the risk-return expectation, and the investment of assets to mitigate risk or enhance return.

– Within an organisation, each legal entity is required to be solvent on a regulatory basis. The capital required by the regulations is intended to ensure that
  – promises to customers are met,
  – there is sufficient capital to meet the expenses in order to manage the business in run-off, and
  – there is a buffer sufficient for the business to withstand an extremely adverse event and have time to take action to prepare the business for run-off such that it would still be able to meet its promises to customers and suppliers.
  The objective of the regulatory basis is to ensure that each legal entity holds sufficient funds to be able to buy the insurance[7] to protect and deliver on the promises made to customers acquired to date. The buffer acts as a trigger point by which the regulator can understand when to get closer to the operation of the business and, if the position cannot be improved, ensure that management can take action in a timely manner to close to new business, derisk the balance sheet through buying the insurance to protect the obligations to existing policyholders as much as possible.
  A Group sets up instruments to ensure that their financial resources can move around the business so that capital is available in each of its

legal entities to meet the regulatory minimum requirements at all times. This requires an actual ability to move capital physically between businesses. This is solvency management.

– Internally, an organisation assesses the capital it needs to hold in order to take risks and make a return. This is an internal economic view of the world that allows for such things as new business growth requirements and credit rating targets. The amount of capital believed to be needed based on this internal assessment is not necessarily the same as that required by the regulatory assessment. Additionally, the internal management structure associated with how an organisation manages its risk exposure may bear no resemblance to the legal entity structure established by regulation. Thus, this tends to be a notional allocation of capital as a budget to back each risk, and is managed through the use of risk limits. This is capital management.

– There is the need to take any capital that is in the hands of the organisation and invest it into some form of financial instrument or asset. The decisions about the investment of capital will have regard to any regulatory restrictions that may apply, the nature of the promises made to customers and suppliers and when these obligations may fall due, the return that can be achieved from each asset class and losses that equally may be brought to bear, and whether the company can afford to take such a risk. This is investment management.

3.4.3.1   *Time out for some simplified examples*

The following examples are used to explain the difference between solvency and capital management. For simplicity, let us assume our management structure and our legal entity structure within the Group are the same.

Assume a Group has one business unit and that the business unit is required to hold £100m of capital for regulatory purposes. The Group may allocate £110m of physical capital to the business unit to meet the regulatory requirements and hold a small buffer to prevent the Group having to inject and withdraw capital on a daily basis as operational performance and stock markets fluctuate.

The risk function has assessed the risks in the business, and on an internal economic basis believes the business unit needs an allocation of economic capital equivalent to 140 per cent of its regulatory requirement, or £140m (equivalent to £100m * 140% = £140m). However, the additional economic capital is not physically moved to the business unit, but is a notional allocation of capital from the Group, the use of which is monitored through the risk limits established to manage the risk-taking of the business unit. These limits are established to ensure the Group, in aggregate, utilises its economic capital optimally, neither overcommitting capital such that its risk to solvency is unacceptable, nor undercommitting capital such that it risks not achieving a competitive return.

Alternatively, the difference between solvency and economic capital can be explained as follows:

Your son's birthday is approaching, and your partner has tasked you to go into town and spend £50 on presents. In your pocket, you have the physical 'bus fare home' and the family's credit card to buy the presents. Having been to town, you return home triumphantly with the presents.

Solvency capital is like the amount of cash in your pocket, the 'bus fare home', while the economic capital is like the credit card, a budget that you have been given to spend.

The cash in your pocket needs to be there to meet the demands of the services you use to get to town. As an individual, you are not concerned with which accounts your partner uses to settle the credit card – you have a budget to spend on presents that does not need to exist as cash in your pocket.

In effect, you are the business unit, and your partner is managing the family's position, the family being equivalent to the Group.

3.4.4   Taxonomy

Frequently, the term 'management of capital' is used too loosely in role profiles, which can lead to confusion and conflict within an organisation. It is necessary for the internal taxonomy to distinguish between management of regulatory solvency through the physical movement of financial resources, management of risk through a notional allocation of economic capital, and the investment of assets[8].

In practice, the task of managing the business based on economic capital cannot be totally isolated from ensuring that all the regulated entities throughout the business are adequately capitalised at all times. Business unit management needs to steer the business using economic capital, while ensuring the solvency level is appropriately maintained within the relevant regulated entities. The closer the organisation is to a single balance sheet, the closer the management of solvency and capital becomes.

3.4.5   Who is concerned with managing which view of capital?

The loose use of the term 'capital' within role profiles and policies can lead to confusion over accountability and responsibility for management. Many people see the differences in the following ways:

1. The Finance team is generally concerned with
   (a) what capital is available,
   (b) how to manage the available capital to meet the regulatory require-
       ments around the legal entities,
   (c) what instruments exist to raise capital,
   (d) what the appropriate mix of capital is, and
   (e) how the cost of the capital base can be lowered.
2. The risk function is concerned with understanding how much capital we
   really need, in the absence of having any supervisory or regulatory framework and how to optimise the return from the risk profile. This is done by
   understanding the implications of the risk profile, the potential returns
   from each risk type, the size and nature of any potential losses, and the
   probability of these losses occurring. This results in the notional allocation of economic capital to each risk, and thus the capital to be taken into
   account in pricing and assessing products and services that give rise to
   these exposures and to measuring business unit performance.

4
Performance Measurement

This chapter provides coverage of the primary risk and return performance measures. In particular, it will show

- the context for the importance of risk and return in decision-making;
- how to distil the primary performance measures from the objectives and expectations of the company's stakeholders;.
- risk-adjusted performance measures relating to plan, profit and return on capital;
- the common risk appetite dimensions and how they can be developed;
- how the delivery of the performance metrics is managed through a risk appetite and limit framework.

4.1 Context

4.1.1 Risk versus return trade-off

Historically, companies have been willing to articulate to external stakeholders the return that they aim to achieve, but they have said little about the risks they are taking to achieve that return.

The recent drive to include statements about risk-taking is about trying to provide a balance of information and to enhance the understanding that achieving a higher return is usually about taking on a higher level of risk. Additionally, the inclusion of information about targets around risk-taking can provide insights into trade-offs where return is being foregone because other key performance or business targets are of a greater priority.

'Mean-variance analysis' has been used to describe plots of return against the amount of risk being taken to achieve that return. A simplified mean-variance framework is illustrated in Figure 4.1.

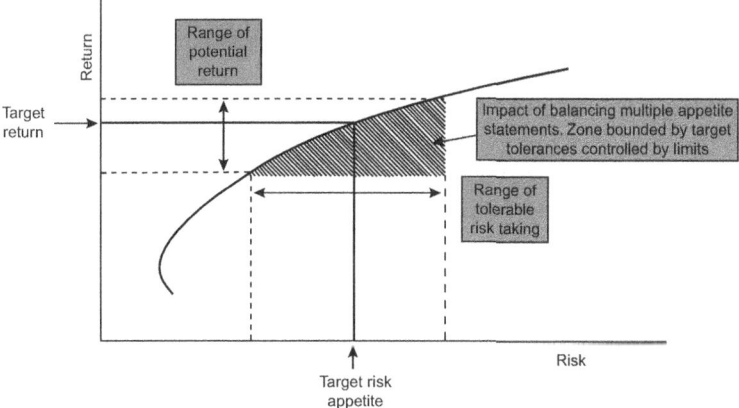

Figure 4.1   A simplified mean-variance framework illustrating risk appetite

The expected return is illustrated on the vertical axis. The term 'risk appetite' has been used to articulate the position on the horizontal axis that represents the amount of risk-taking being targeted. In setting a strategy, a company may be willing to accept some volatility in the expected return, for which it is willing to allow the amount of risk-taking to fluctuate within certain bounds or limits. This is also important because the actual expected return and amount of risk-taking do change over time as the economic circumstances and business mix change. Therefore, being able to provide this framework and set of boundaries helps one to manage the organisation on a day-to-day basis in a more dynamic way without continuously referring to the Board for approvals or needing to take actions daily that could damage long-term market credibility.

The curve provides the 'frontier' that illustrates the optimum return achievable for different amounts of risk being taken based on the strategies available. The frontier is determined by making assumptions about the expected return and expected amount of risk from the various strategies that are possible. One of the key assumptions concerns how the risks from these strategies interact.

It is not possible to get a position above the line because this would represent achieving a higher return from the same amount of risk. Moving the curve may be achieved by adding other strategies with different levels of return and risk profile.

It is possible to choose a mix of investments or strategies that is below the line, or sub-optimal. This may be a result of having multiple risk appetite statements that create additional constraints that this simple representation does not cater for.

However, the performance of an organisation is not solely measurable in these two dimensions – this is a simplified picture. There are a number of elements that need to be considered when assessing the upside performance objectives and the downside possibilities from adverse events materialising.

The Board determines a company strategy based on balancing the objectives of its various stakeholders. The objectives of the various stakeholders provide the targets and the constraints within which this performance must be delivered. Based on the agreed strategy, a set of objectives is determined. At each level of the organisation, the objectives are converted into a delivery plan. The delivery plan of the superior provides the basis for establishing the objectives for the subordinate, and so on until the organisation's objectives have been cascaded throughout the various levels and teams. This approach ensures that the overarching strategic objectives and risk appetite cascade through the company to ensure those on the 'frontline' can see clearly how what they do aligns with delivering the strategy and why the limits within which they work help control the overall outcome.

For example, the executives convert their objectives into a delivery plan, which forms the basis of the objectives of their managers, who in turn develop a plan for how to deliver their objectives. The managers' plans form the basis for the objectives of their staff, who then develop plans as to how they will deliver their objectives.

4.1.2   The business model

As outlined in Section 3, in order to shape the strategic objectives, it is useful for an organisation to articulate its business model. The business model outlines what the business does and how it makes money in doing it. This articulation helps stakeholders, both internally and externally, to understand where the return is expected to come from and the sort of risks the business is expected to take.

If a large loss arises from an event or investment that is out of line with the activities and expectations articulated through the business model, there are rightly going to be some difficult questions to answer. Conversely, if the loss arises from activities within the scope of the business model, the explanations are somewhat easier, even if the loss remains difficult to swallow.

For example, an insurance business in France writing motor business in France may find it difficult to explain insolvency arising directly from investments relating to sub-prime mortgage lending in the United States.

4.1.3 An organisation's stakeholders

Stakeholders are the groups that have an interest in what the company achieves and how it goes about achieving it.

Different stakeholders have different underlying motivations for this interest. An organisation's various stakeholder groups may include

- debtholders and rating agencies,
- shareholders and investment analysts,
- regulators and supervisors,
- governments,
- customers,
- staff and management,
- other stakeholders, such as the wider society.

4.1.3.1 *Debtholders[1] and rating agencies*

Debtholders provide an organisation with funding in the form of a loan, and are mainly interested in ensuring the continued ability of the organisation to make agreed interest payments and generate sufficient return to be able to repay the loan when this falls due. As the debt will rank behind the policyholder and other obligations (but ahead of equity) generally, there is an underlying desire for the organisation to maintain a safety buffer above the minimum amount of capital that is required to remain solvent and be able to meet all its obligations when they fall due. Ideally, debtholders like an equity stakeholder to exist. This is because, if the company looked increasingly likely to fail, then it would default on the equity first, ahead of the debt. Hence, the equity stakeholder is likely to have actively engaged the company early to find a solution to prevent a corporate failure ahead of reaching a point at which the equity capital has been 'burnt through' (defaulted on) and the company's debt instruments become 'at risk'. These discussions will have occurred and investigations been undertaken ahead of the interests of debtholders being adversely impacted.

Rating agencies provide a service for debtholders by providing a guide to the ability of the organisation to meet its debt obligations. This includes assessing a company's financial strength and stability, its ability to service the cash flow demands of debtholders, and its risk management capabilities.

These stakeholder groups are keen on good risk management and a degree of stability in profits to provide security to the potential cash flow demands of the debt instruments. As has been evidenced with the UK government credit rating downgrades in 2013, the rating agencies like to see businesses delivering on their growth plans and see evidence of action taken to mitigate risk in an effective and timely manner.

4.1.3.2   Shareholders and investment analysts

Shareholders invest capital into a company with the view that they will receive both a dividend stream and an increase in the value of their capital investment. This means shareholders have a number of interests:

(a) The company has sufficient money to grow the business in line with the plan.
(b) Ideally, shareholders would like a steady and increasing value of dividend payments over time. As the determinant of the dividend is the income that is left after all the other stakeholders have been paid, shareholders are interested in this measure of profitability and its variability over time. If there are limits and constraints that bite before dividends can be declared, shareholders are keen to ensure an organisation can meet these.
(c) Shareholders want to ensure that the company has sufficient liquid assets to pay its dividends in cash when they fall due. As shareholders will rank behind meeting cash requirements to pay claims, shareholders will be interested in the liquidity of assets and the cash generation considerations of the business.

Profitability stems from the organisation's taking risk; if the company were only going to achieve a risk-free return, there would not be any point in the shareholders putting money into the organisation just to take the risk that they would not get it back. Additionally, it may be that this rather pointless return is also taxed twice before it reaches the pockets of the investor – once as profit in the company and secondly as income when it reaches the hands of the investor.

The loss of control over money being invested and being taxed twice is the reason why shareholders do not value a business doing things that the shareholder could do directly. These issues are discussed further in Section 4.2.5.

Shareholders expect an organisation to take risks aligned with the business that it is in and to earn a fair return for taking those risks. The nature of the organisation's business and the statements that it has made will create expectations for shareholders of what return and risks they can expect the company to take. Shareholders will expect companies in similar sectors writing similar business mixes to take similar risks and earn similar returns.

This is the case unless the company can articulate its reasons for being different and explain how this repositions their risk-return profile relative to competitors.

4.1.3.3 Regulators and supervisors

Primarily, regulators are concerned with customer protection and that, with a reasonable degree of certainty, a company will be able to meet its obligations as they fall due. This means, not only a view of the organisation's financial strength but also its liquidity requirements.

Regulators are also interested in the way in which the organisation operates with respect to its customers to ensure that organisations are being fair to their customers in the way that they do business with them.

For example, a financial services regulator may have the following objectives:

– enabling confidence to be maintained in the financial system and the functioning of the market functions, providing a continuity of service to the public;
– protecting and enhancing the integrity of the financial system, and thus minimising the use of the market for the purposes of committing financial crime;
– promoting protection for current and future customers;
– promoting competition within the market for the benefit of customers.

4.1.3.4 Governments and taxpayers

Governments have objectives to ensure that

– sectors remain competitive;
– there is financial stability in the economic system;
– the treasury receives stable and increasing tax revenues from diverse sources;
– employment levels are maintained, and reliance on government benefits is minimised;
– companies do not damage the reputation of the country and any of its material trading partners;
– companies provide products that fill the gaps between government provision and the basic needs of individuals at various stages in life.

Governments can use legislation to control how its objectives are met, and in a crisis can, to some extent, act as a guarantor of last resort to underpin the security of a sector by bailing out institutions in crisis. However, this is achieved by redirecting tax revenues from other services or increasing revenue from other sources such as taxpayers and consumers. Therefore, the value of doing this needs to be balanced against the downside impacts in other areas.

Therefore, governments are keen on ensuring that organisations avoid suffering large losses or are able to withstand a certain level of market volatility to avoid an additional burden on the taxpayers in adverse times. Having achieved this, the government is interested in companies' medium- to long-term viability and their ability to write profitable business year-on-year that encourages consumer spending, and thus supports the government's future tax revenue stream.

4.1.3.5   Customers

Customers take out policies or contracts that create expectations about what the company will do in various circumstances. In general, customers want products and services that are a good value for the money, and companies that are easy to do business with, clear in the information and expectations that they provide, and that do what they say they will do, including settling up in a reasonable and timely fashion.

4.1.3.6   Staff and management

The majority of staff want to be treated fairly and with respect by their employer and colleagues. They hope that their salary will keep pace with inflation and that they will receive a reasonable level of job security and potential for career progression. Furthermore, some staff would like some element of bonus in recognition of their performance, even in adverse circumstances, if the losses arise from events that they believe were outside of their control.

4.1.3.7   Other stakeholders

A number of organisations apply consideration to the wider social and environmental stakeholders, as their role is to deliver more than just a financial performance. These social considerations may include 'serving the unserved', providing employment, controlling a carbon footprint or investing ethically.

4.1.3.8   Aggregating the objectives and expectations

Table 4.1 provides a summary of stakeholder objectives and expectations. As the executive is charged with delivering the strategy with due regard to the objectives and expectations of all stakeholders, the stakeholder objectives shape the performance objectives and parameters within which the executive

Table 4.1 Summary of stakeholder objectives and expectations

Stakeholders	Performance	What are you aiming to risk?
Debtholders & rating agencies	Make profits sufficient to make interest payments Enough growth to provide the security of the return of the loan that they have made	Cash available to make payments when they fall due Not too much volatility of earnings such that it risks being able to make the payments that are due
Shareholders & investment analysts	Appropriate return on their capital for taking the risks associated with the business. A return commensurate with that from a peer group Growth in the value of the franchise to provide growth in the value of their investment in case they choose to sell it on Make profits sufficient to pay a dividend	Buffer over regulatory capital to be able to write new business and grow the franchise Not too much volatility of earnings such that there is too much risk to the dividend being paid Not take actions that would damage the reputation of the organisation and damage the franchise
Regulators & supervisors	Want companies to grow, but not more than the balance sheet can take	Companies to maintain a buffer over regulatory capital to ensure continued competition and reduce the possibility of breaching regulatory requirements Want companies to behave with integrity towards their consumers and not do things that would damage the reputation of the sector, reducing consumer confidence
Governments & taxpayers	Sell products and services to generate consumer spending, profits for businesses and thus, tax revenues for the government	Buffer over regulatory capital to ensure the companies can grow Not to do things that would damage the reputation of the sector
Customers	Good value products Companies that are easy to do business with Some profit-sharing contracts may expect a certain return and limited volatility of that return	Cash available to pay claims as and when they fall due Want companies to in a way to ensure obligations to customers are secure
Staff & management	Want to be able to operationally deliver the strategic plan to secure bonuses	Buffer over regulatory capital to ensure the continued growth of the business to secure long-term employment Cash available to pay salaries and other benefits

is required to deliver the strategy for the company. From this picture, a Board needs to distil the primary performance objectives and develop a framework for how it is going to control its risks in achieving those objectives.

4.2   Performance measurement – return

4.2.1   What are the questions that the Board should ask?

With respect to upside performance, the questions the Board could consider include

1. Which measures drive decision-making about our performance and which are constraints on what we do?
2. Are we adding value for our investors?
3. Are we making an economic profit?
4. Which parts of the business are making profit?
5. How are they making profit?
6. Can we make the same profit by taking less risk?
7. Are we allocating our capital efficiently to optimise the opportunities available to us?
8. If we have excess capital, to which business unit should it be given?
9. If we are capital constrained, what is the most efficient way to reduce risk-taking?
10. How diverse are the set of opportunities in which we are invested?
11. What is the sensitivity of our profit streams and to which events are they most exposed?
12. What opportunities and return are we foregoing in following our strategy?

4.2.2   Background

With rafts of information in a Board room, it can become difficult for Board members to understand which measures and metrics are meant to be driving decision-making and which are aspects that are constraints, or ways in which the market measures things that will need explaining. Over time, as the fortunes of the business change, it may be that some of the measures that are constraints become more prominent in constraining decisions that a Board would otherwise like to take if it could adopt a pure economic rationale. For example, a situation could arise in which liquidity becomes a constraint on a company's ability to settle claims, at which point it would become a constraint on making decisions on a purely economic basis. This constraint on liquidity could equally be a result of a company being successful and writing too much business, as it is investing in a way that means assets cannot be realised without a significant haircut to the valuation.

> Effectively, in writing a policy, an insurer converts liquid cash into an asset defined by a stream of future profits which is thus less liquid. This means that growing the business can lead to a material reduction in available liquid assets on the balance sheet, even when the balance sheet appears financially strong. This is why an understanding of the velocity of cash (the speed with which cash goes out to work and profits are realised back into cash terms) is extremely important.

We find that strong long-term sustainable businesses decide on what is going to constitute the target for its performance objectives based on the true underlying economics of the business. There may be decisions made to write some business on a more aggressive basis, but this is then underpinned by an explicit understanding of why the company is willing to deviate from this target performance level and the implications.

Historically, many businesses faced with excessive growth opportunities or competition have tried to justify chasing business at ever less justifiable prices because of concerns over their image in the marketplace relative to that of competitors. The bubble in Collateralised Debt Obligations (CDOs[2]) ahead of the credit crisis was an example of companies chasing market share without a real understanding of the shortcomings of parameters used in pricing. The presence and subsequent bursting of bubbles in markets illustrates why market share and position are not the best performance measure, as they represent the chasing of the emotion of a market, which is not necessarily driven by economic reality.

As the chief executive officer (CEO) is under constant pressure to grow the business in line with peers, when a market segment is starting to grow at a significant rate, there are some important questions:

– Does the CEO know which part of the business is making the most profit and why?
– Is the area of growth one in which no directly relevant information was available to assess the risks?
– Is the amount of risk being assumed based on arbitraging models used internally or by those with whom trades are being placed?

CEOs need to be able to communicate the fundamental economic position on which they are growing their business and why some opportunities do not make rational business sense to be pursued. 'Knowing your business' is about knowing the economics of your business and when not to chase segments because they are priced unrealistically.

> Sometimes the best thing you can do is just go to the golf course and do absolutely nothing for a bit. – Warren Buffet

This is extremely difficult to do if you are a new CEO trying to build a credible reputation within a sector. The emotion that underpins investor decisions can make the market take short-term views that impact executive careers before a CEO's position is proven to be correct. Enhancing communication and understanding for stakeholders becomes critical. We need

– a framework that articulates the primary performance measures that drive the business and enables the other metrics to be seen as 'constraints' on ensuring the business is managing all its stakeholder demands;
– primary metrics that are easy to explain and understand;
– a way to explain the parameters we use within these metrics and why they should be set at the levels we do.

4.2.3   Developing the primary performance measures

Once stakeholders have achieved satisfaction that the company meets all the minimum criteria (constraints), they may have the following primary performance interests:

1. Stakeholders want to grow a profitable franchise to build on the value of the business the company has today.
   The assessment of the value of the company should reflect a value placed on the assets and the business that the company has now, and an amount to reflect the additional value someone would place on the company's ability to create additional profits from its new business generating capability, should he or she want to buy the company. This value should be based on a realistic assessment of the potential profits that may arise, rather than a basis determined by prescriptive regulation that would include prudent margins and misrepresent the profits we should expect.
2. Providers of capital will be keen to understand the true economics of the business and the realistic potential profits that could occur over

time and thus, the likely income they may receive and return on capital invested.

3. In order to optimise the reward for the risks being taken, stakeholders will benefit from an understanding of how this capital is being allocated to achieve best economic use.

This means that the stakeholders will be interested in a number of key financial measures:

- enhancing the enterprise value by growing the franchise (enterprise value);
- the amount of value created in economic terms (risk-adjusted value creation);
- a measure of the return achieved on the capital being used (risk-adjusted return on lifetime economic capital).

These measures need to incorporate some important attributes:

- be based on a realistic economic view.
- reflect the risks being taken to earn the return.
- be usable, such that they are simple enough to be explained and managed.
- support business planning and set targets against which actual performance can be evaluated.
- provide reasonable, consistent comparisons of diverse business opportunities across a company and the returns that can be made.

4.2.4   First primary performance measure – enterprise value

The enterprise value of a company is determined from a realistic projection of the future cash flows that shareholders should expect to receive from the company's assets and from its current and future business. This forward-looking view of a company means that initiatives to increase the value of new business today have implications, not just for the coming year but potentially for years into the future. This approach would be consistent with that used to assess an investment in a new product launch or other initiative, and that used in business planning.

Effectively, the enterprise value is determined from three key elements:

- the net value of the assets that belong to shareholders and have been accumulated to date;

- the value attached to profits that are expected to arise and be transferred to shareholders in the future from business that has been written to date;
- a value for the potential profits that could arise and be transferred to shareholders in the future from business that will be written over the coming years.

The enterprise value is a guide to the value of the business and formulaically.[3]

> *Enterprise value = value of net assets + the present value of the expected transfer to shareholders from in-force business + Goodwill*

Goodwill is the present value of the profits that could arise and be transferred to shareholders in the future from business that will be written over the coming years.

There are various ways of assessing the value of goodwill, particularly using the information from the business plan. However, a quick, simple to understand and pragmatic approach to determining the value of goodwill is from the present value of profits from new business written in the coming year scaled up by a multiplier. This multiplier is a view of the number of years new business generating capability that should be allowed for in the assessment. In some markets, the concept of the multiplier is still used by analysts. Alternatively, it could be

- inferred from market data about the prices paid for acquisitions relative to the immediate value of the company,
- inferred and approximated from business plan projections and changes in company value, or
- based on some mathematical models that have been developed from which a value can be inferred.

An assessment of an appropriate multiplier should determine a value based on long-term levels and not be subject to regular change (particularly if market data or views of investment analysts are being used). Analyst views and current market data will provide a guide to the current market conditions and sentiment towards the company. The current level of a new business multiplier below the long-term level would indicate either a bad time to sell a business (and a good time to buy), or a need to communicate to and manage the understanding of external stakeholders about the position and strategy that the company is pursuing.

The present value of the expected future transfers to shareholders from in-force business and new business used in the enterprise value calculation would be consistent with the Risk-Adjusted Value Creation metric outlined in Section 4.2.5.

The benefit of the enterprise value measure is that any assessment of a proposed strategy is presented relative to its impact on the whole value of the organisation and as a longer-term investment through the impact on goodwill, rather than as an isolated one-off event.

As with all measures, one of the key insights is to understand the drivers of the sensitivity of this measure. The questions should not stop at 'the measure is sensitive to the new business multiplier', for example, but go on to achieve an understanding of what would drive the changes to the multiplier and what historic experience of fluctuations exists to support this assessment.

4.2.5   Second primary performance measure – risk-adjusted value created

A business grows as genuine economic value is created, but the question remains: How is economic value created in the eyes of an investor?

An investor provides money to a company in order for it to create absolute value through undertaking activities that the investor cannot undertake directly, and to ensure that he or she is no worse off as a result of incurring any additional costs such as additional taxation charges. The value that is created needs to be sufficient to compensate the investor for the risks that he or she is taking with the capital and the control of the investment being passed to management. A risk-adjusted value creation (RAVC) measure determines the economic profit adjusted for the costs of the risks being taken.

RAVC = economic profit – expected return for taking market risk – frictional cost of capital

As an absolute measure, with explicit adjustments for risk, if RAVC is greater than 0, there is value being created for the shareholder (that is, the appropriate hurdle for performance purposes is 0).

The components of RAVC can be thought of as follows:

1. Economic profit is the profit made in the period assessed on an economic basis and is generally extracted from the change in capital available on the balance sheet over the period being considered.

In this form, RAVC can be used for planning and pricing purposes through using information about the profits that are expected to emerge, and also for actual performance evaluation by using information relating to profits that have actually emerged over the period.

To assess the potential future RAVC as part of the business-planning process, one can extract the results from the cash flow projections that are provided. However, if the projections are based on projecting a regulatory balance sheet forward over a period of time, there may be areas of prudence, prescription or basis of calculation in the regulatory assessment that are not consistent with an economic view. These differences should fall as 'margin releases' into the cash flows in each year, and thus be brought through the economic profit calculation. For example, a regulatory balance sheet may prescribe that it is prepared assuming that the organisation ceases to accept new business after one year and thus, there may be different assumptions about expense inflation between a projection assuming a business continues to write new business which contributes to overhead costs, and one that is required to close and not obtain economies of scale.

2. Expected return for taking market risk deducts the expected return present in the economic profit that results from investing in 'risky' assets.

    If a shareholder can invest directly into financial markets (for example shares), he or she can achieve a risk-free return plus a premium for taking risk without involving the company. A company adds no value by doing something a shareholder could do him- or herself. Hence, any profits that are included that arise from activities that a shareholder could have undertaken and achieved without the company need to be removed.

    For example, if a company invests £100 in gilts with an expected return of 3 per cent, it only creates economic value if its profits exceed this 3 per cent expected return. Equally, if the £100 is invested in risky assets with an expected return of 6 per cent, the company only creates value if it generates profits in excess of this 6 per cent expected return. Hence, in order to assess the company's economic value add, we need to adjust the economic profit figure for the expected returns from the underlying market risks that are being taken.

    Whether to pursue a higher return-higher risk or lower return-lower risk approach is a strategic business decision that is not based on one of these approaches being of greater economic value.

3. Frictional cost of capital is a measure of the additional return that shareholders expect to receive for providing capital and giving up control of their assets to management and suffering additional charges such as tax on returns. Examples of the frictional costs are

(a) double-taxation: the return that is earned by a company is first taxed at the company tax rate. Any dividends declared from this post-tax profit are then taxed again when the shareholder receives them. Thus, shareholders who provide funds to a company expect a return that compensates them for this 'drag' on their return as well as for the risks they take with the funds.

(b) principal-agent issues: effectively, investors hire the management team to deliver the strategic ambition of the company in the interests of stakeholders. However, there is a risk that management will not always act in their best interests, or will take risks that the shareholders did not expect. For example, management may seek excessive pay awards for generating revenue without considering the economics of the business being written or properly assessing the risks being taken. The value that shareholders place on these 'agency costs' will depend on factors such as their assessment of the quality of management and transparency with which the company is run.[4] These factors mean that it is difficult to quantify objectively the value of agency costs, but studies suggest that it is a function of the amount of capital or cash flow.

The frictional cost of capital is determined by applying a charge for the cost of capital to the amount of economic capital being targeted. The charge for the cost of capital is a subjective assessment and has usually been within the range of 2.5 per cent to 6 per cent p.a., with the average being around 4 per cent p.a.

Developing metrics in this way means that the adjustments for the expected return and frictional costs are different from the traditional hurdle rate approach (that is, discounting the cash flows at a higher hurdle rate, for example 12 per cent pa, to make an approximate adjustment for risk). While it is possible for the traditional flat hurdle rate approach to give results in aggregate analogous to the method above, the approach is not representative of the risks being run when a more granular analysis of the business is being performed in which not all products or business lines are giving rise to the same profile of risks. The traditional flat approach can, therefore, when looking through to the underlying sources of risk and return, give rise to the potential for flawed decision-making. The traditional flat hurdle rate approach creates difficulty for business units trying to understand what actions they can take to improve their risk-adjusted performance and hence can limit risk-return optimisation decisions. The approach also becomes ineffective when there have been major changes in the business model, where the hurdle rate may no longer be an appropriate reflection of the aggregate risk profile from which it was generated.

The RAVC measure is transparent in the nature of the risk adjustments made, and allows for risk directly, which means it can be more usefully applied at the granular portfolio level to manage the sources of risk exposures.

4.2.5.1   The application of RAVC to new business

When RAVC is determined from all expected future cash flows from the start of a contract, it provides a new business profitability assessment within pricing activity, which for convenience, can be called the risk-adjusted value of new business (RAVNB). As for RAVC, a positive RAVNB translates into value creation for shareholders.

4.2.6   Third primary performance measure – risk-adjusted return on lifetime economic capital (RARLEC)

The amount of capital available to a company is limited, and thus decisions need to be made as to how to allocate it between the various opportunities that have been presented. The Board wants to understand why the collection of opportunities being pursued utilises the total capital available in a way that optimises the expected return. It is important to establish a measure that enables them to understand whether a better overall return can be achieved through the reallocation of capital to different opportunities.[5] For this, we need a risk-adjusted return on capital measure that can be applied in a consistent manner across various opportunities. The complexity with some types of business is that the capital is not put out to work for one year, returned and the opportunities re-assessed at the next planning round for capital to be re-allocated. Some products once written, tie up capital for a prolonged period of time over which it is steadily released. Hence, the return measure needs to allow for this lifetime over which the capital is used.[6]

The risk-adjusted return on lifetime economic capital (RARLEC) is a relative measure of economic value and capital efficiency, the primary purpose of which is to assist in making decisions about allocating capital efficiently between new opportunities.

4.2.6.1   Definition of RARLEC

RARLEC is defined as

RARLEC = RAVNB/Present value of Lifetime Economic Capital requirements.

RARLEC is akin to a risk-adjusted return on capital measure, and quantifies how much risk-adjusted value is created relative to the amount of lifetime economic capital that is required.

What is lifetime economic capital? Contracts are written in terms that mean they may remain in force over an extended period of time, sometimes many years (for example, a term assurance policy may last ten years, and a motor policy just over one year[7]). Over this period of time, the business is required to hold economic capital to back the risks to which the business remains exposed. The amount of economic capital does not remain constant over this period, but varies as the exposure to the risks varies. Hence, the present value of economic capital requirements is used to reflect the fact that contracts may continue for many years with different levels of capital required in each of the future years.

This also means that when assessing business opportunities and how to allocate capital efficiently, the duration over which the capital will be 'tied-up' needs to be considered when making comparisons of the potential return between opportunities (for example, considering the return earned on a motor policy of term one year against the return on a term assurance policy of ten years). It is not as simple as assuming that shorter term contracts will continue to achieve the same level of return into the future. Consideration needs to be given to factors such as market cycles and competitive pressures that may result in profit levels not being maintained.

As RARLEC uses the output from RAVC (or more precisely, RAVNB), the assessment of capital efficiency naturally aligns with the assessment of value creation outlined in Section 4.2.5.

4.2.6.2 Secondary measures

Having defined the primary performance measures, it remains necessary to monitor other measures, including those that the external market uses to assess businesses and compare across companies. This ensures that the impact of economic decisions on metrics used by other parties can be explained.

4.2.7 Issues for consideration when using economic capital within metrics

Risk measurement through the calculation of economic capital is, by its nature, a backward-looking assessment of the amount of capital that would have been needed under previous circumstances (that is, it is derived from assessing information and data relating to past periods and events). It is likely that few adjustments have been made to the amount of economic capital required to reflect the potential future evolution of risks, and thus, the longer the projection into the future, the less accurate the historic assessment of the required amount of economic capital will become.

For example, if the product is of a term of 1 year or less, the capital assessment may be reasonable. However, if the product has a term of 30 years, the assessment of the capital required in 29 years' time based on information known today will be less accurate, as it will not incorporate the additional 29 years of experience.

As an example, though based on financial market risk, data on which the amount of capital has been determined to back credit risk will have been adversely impacted by the events of 2008–2010, particularly for financial institutions. Thus, when making decisions to invest in credit for the medium- to long term going forward, the prospective view of the risk-adjusted return will not reflect any changes to the approach to managing and regulating financial institutions that has occurred subsequent to the crisis. There will need to be an application of expert judgment about the future.

This highlights why any performance measures are only guides and not the single absolute correct answer.

Additionally, the assessment of the economic capital requirements will make assumptions about how risks being taken interact and the benefit that arises from pursuing a diverse range of potential return-generating opportunities. It is important that the method of allocating this benefit from diversification back to risks that give rise to the benefit, is able to do so in a reasonable manner. This is because opportunities that are of a significant enough size to change the benefit from diversification need to be fully understood, as changes in diversification benefit may have implications for the risk-adjusted return on capital beyond the products they impact directly.

4.3   Performance measurement – risk appetite

4.3.1   Questions for the Board

The following questions can help shape the thinking about risk appetite:

1. How much risk do we aim to take in order to achieve the return?
2. What are we willing to risk in order to achieve the objectives?
3. How do these align with our stakeholders' objectives?
4. What capital will we need to meet our growth trajectory over the next five years?
5. What cash do we need to support business growth over the next five years?

6. What is the impact of new business on the evolution of our risk profile over the next five years? Will this change the likely level of volatility of results we expect?
7. What issues would cause us to worry and how likely are they to happen?
   - for example, a credit rating downgrade, the need to issue a profits warning, an inability to meet cash outflows or invest in new initiatives, or customers and distributors becoming disillusioned with the way we do business.

4.3.2 Introduction

Having defined the upside performance measures in Section 4.2, it is necessary to understand how these will be managed to ensure they are delivered within an acceptable range of outcomes, and how trade-offs to any non-financial aspects will be monitored to ensure these are delivered also. In this regard, the term 'risk appetite' is not wholly helpful.

We are looking to establish an acceptable range within which the Board is satisfied that management can deliver the performance objectives given the vagaries of the market as we know it today. The aim is to deliver the performance objectives based on a target amount of risk-taking – the risk appetite – but there is an acceptance that things happen and the outturn can be other than expected, meaning that results can fluctuate over time. Thus, the Board is willing to accept deviation from the risk appetite to an agreed extent to allow management to function efficiently day to day and not have to operate in a manner that requires continuous referral to a higher committee for actions to be approved.

However, there are limits to this tolerance, in particular for delegated decision-making, for which the Board will need to establish points at which management need to engage at higher levels in the organisation to seek approval for certain actions.

The most common definition of risk appetite appears to go along the following lines:

> Risk appetite is the *maximum amount of risk* an undertaking is *willing* to accept in order to achieve its strategic objectives. This global amount will then act as the root of all risk management processes and limits that will be cascaded throughout the daily operations.

We believe this could be slightly misleading. The 'maximum amount of risk' or 'the amount of risk a company is willing to take' determines a boundary or tolerance rather than a target amount of risk that a company is aiming to take to achieve its performance objectives. This target amount is more aligned with the risk appetite. Thus, we would restate the definition as:

> Risk appetite reflects the target level of uncertainty of outcome that an undertaking is *aiming* to accept in order to achieve its strategic objectives. This position will then act as the root of all risk management processes and targets that will be cascaded throughout the daily operations.

This approach helps position risk appetite as the strategic medium-term aim, and the risk tolerances and limits as the tactical short-term target ranges.

4.3.2.1   Benefits of a risk appetite framework

If risk appetite is to be a valuable medium-term strategic ambition that drives future risk-reward decision-making in the business, its effectiveness rests on how well it is understood throughout the organisation and used within organisational processes, starting with strategy and business planning.

For the risk appetite framework to add value to a business, it needs to do the following:

- It must support the clear understanding of how stakeholder objectives and the business plan are aligned and managed, thus reducing the likelihood of unpleasant surprises for all concerned;
- It must align with the metrics for managing the business so that the Board's information requirements are clearly understood. In this way, the communication and insights provided by management about the business and its issues can be targeted to be clearly relevant. This clearer understanding of the linkage between business objectives and the management of risk can positively influence behaviours.
- It must be translated into ranges that are relevant to the current position of the organisation and able to be adjusted over time to ensure continued delivery over the medium term, the period over which the risk appetite is being assessed and monitored.
- It must provide managers with an understanding of what risk management means to their roles and the boundaries within which they can operate. This can enhance the company's ability to take on risk, as the capacity to do so is about more than just a financial capacity to absorb losses. A company's ability to understand what constitutes an acceptable

exposure and how to manage it is critical to its risk-taking capability. This ability to manage risk is about having the skills and experience coupled with the necessary controls and infrastructure.

Consider, at the JP Morgan AGM in 2013, its directors stated that the bank's risk committee could not be blamed for failing to spot the London Whale scandal, which cost it $6.2bn (£4.1bn) last year, because if the derivatives trades were too complex for the people who put them together to understand, the Board could not be expected to understand them either.

– It must be expressed in a way that people can understand and translate into useable performance objectives for each member of the staff such that they are incentivised to deliver performance within acceptable bounds that meet the organisation's overall objectives.

Clearly articulating the risk appetite statements in external communications can assist in managing investors and other external stakeholders, as transparency and understanding of the risk that a company is taking to deliver its performance objectives can enhance management's credibility, and may lead to a reduction in the volatility of the share price resulting from market sentiment.

4.3.2.2 *Proposed set of primary risk appetite metrics*

Section 4.2 outlined the primary return metrics based on stakeholder expectations. We use the same approach for the risk appetite statements to ensure the framework reflects the drivers of the primary return metrics and thus, stakeholder expectations. This gives rise to the following dimensions:

– capital adequacy
– earnings volatility
– liquidity
– franchise value[8]

If we monitor and manage the elements that impact these risk appetite dimensions, through the direct linkage of these dimensions to the primary performance objectives, we are monitoring and managing the drivers of our performance objectives.

In developing the short-term tactical limit framework for these dimensions (usually through red, amber and green, or RAG limits), we establish how much volatility in our performance we are willing to accept. In developing these boundaries, we need to consider that both too much and too little risk can damage the performance and perception of an organisation. Simply put, for example, risk-adjusted return is earnings divided by capital. Too much capital will cause a drag on the risk-adjusted return. A continued drag on performance can be a risk to the business, as fewer investors may be willing to supply capital to the business in order to support its growth, which could depress the share price (based on supply-and-demand dynamics) and weaken the financial position. Additionally, pressure may be brought to bear to return, what is seen as, excess capital to shareholders.

Feedback from a number of multinationals suggest that shareholders equally do not like the surprise of too much profit as too little, as it can be unnerving and undermine the perception of management's understanding of the business and the credibility of business plans.

4.3.3   First risk appetite dimension – capital adequacy

4.3.3.1   Approach for calibrating the capital risk appetite statement

Setting the level of the required amount of capital the business needs is not an exact science. The calibration process requires subjective judgment to determine an appropriate level of capital buffer, usually referred to as the economic capital requirement.

Companies develop business plans that involve investing capital to grow the business and being able to withstand reasonably adverse events without having to curtail the business activities substantially. As well as having capital available when they need it to grow the business, it is necessary for companies to attract investors with an attractive potential rate of return on their investment. If the amount of capital held is too high, the return on this capital will, conversely, be too low, and the company's ability to attract investment at a reasonable price will be difficult. Additionally, as the pricing of products depends on the charge for using the capital that is required, the higher the capital requirement, the higher the price of the product. High capital requirements could result in the products becoming uncompetitive, which could be equally damaging for the long-term viability of the business.

Conversely, if investors see the risks to their investment as being high, the compensation they will want for investing in the company will be high. If the cost of raising capital is higher than the return that can be achieved from writing new business, it may not be appropriate or even possible to raise capital and continue to grow the business.

In extremis, operating a company at the minimum capital level set by the regulator can result in various issues:

– There can be an increased demand on management resources to ensure that the financial position remains above the minimum hurdle as the day-to-day fluctuations in stock markets or profits (and losses) impact the balance sheet position. This will also give rise to higher costs associated with more frequent discussions with stakeholders to manage the relationships, such as with the regulator to ensure customers are being appropriately protected.

– There can be a risk that the capital position affects the level of new business generated as customers, distributors and suppliers may become concerned about the ability to meet commitments in the longer term. For general insurance companies, some brokers will only deal with companies of at least an 'A' rating. For reinsurers, some insurers will only deal with reinsurers of at least a 'AA' rating. These are levels higher than the regulatory minimum.

– There can be a higher risk of a requirement to close to new business when the capital position deteriorates, or of the organisation having to take actions that adversely impact the ability to develop the business in the longer term.

– Dividends to external parties may be difficult to justify given the financial outlook for the company.

– There may be a risk that the regulator believes it appropriate to take action against the directors of the company regarding the manner in which they were running it, which may include personal fines, if the financial position permanently deteriorates.

In general, the conclusion companies reach is that a buffer of capital over and above the minimum required to be held by the regulators would be preferable.

To calibrate the capital statement, a number of inputs are considered to gain market and internal perspectives, including

– the risk of breaching the regulatory capital requirements,
– the internal economic capital requirement to deliver the plan,
– benchmarking to ensure the company is not too far out of line with its peers,
– rating agency perspective, and the impact on the cost of raising capital,
– the company's own current and historical capital cover ratios,
– impact on earnings, the stability of earnings and financial strength,

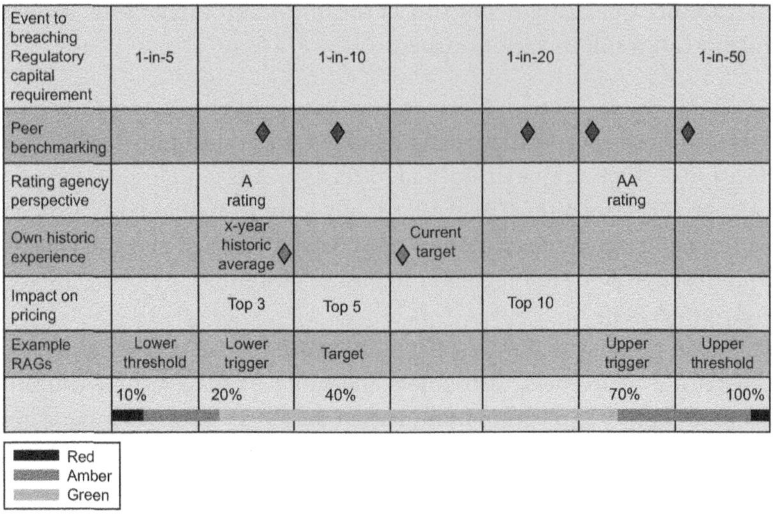

Event to breaching Regulatory capital requirement	1-in-5		1-in-10		1-in-20		1-in-50
Peer benchmarking		◆	◆		◆	◆	◆
Rating agency perspective		A rating				AA rating	
Own historic experience		x-year historic average ◆		Current ◆ target			
Impact on pricing		Top 3	Top 5		Top 10		
Example RAGs	Lower threshold	Lower trigger	Target			Upper trigger	Upper threshold
	10%	20%	40%			70%	100%

Red
Amber
Green

Figure 4.2   Aggregation of the considerations in establishing the capital adequacy risk appetite statement

- the impact of required capital levels on product pricing,
- the number of management actions that are included within the calculation of the financial position and the number of actions still available that are not.

Figure 4.2 illustrates how these different perspectives could be aggregated to provide a framework for discussion and finalising the capital risk appetite calibration.

4.3.3.2   *Overview of capital dimension calibration inputs*

It should be noted that the final decision will not be a result of precise science. Rather, the final risk appetite statement will be a position with which the Board feels comfortable and which is informed by relevant information upon which it has come to a subjective conclusion. The following sections discuss various inputs to the decision making process.

4.3.3.3   *Regulatory capital requirements*

Knowledge of the regulatory capital requirement is paramount to understanding the minimum capital requirements, the frequency with which this position may be breached, and the associated difficulties that may arise. A buffer over the regulatory capital requirements is desirable to ensure the business resources can remain focussed on growing the franchise and that there is sufficient capital available to grow the business in line with the plan without this plan being materially impacted by reasonably foreseeable adverse fluctuations in financial position.

4.3.3.4   *Internal economic capital requirements*

Economic capital is the amount of capital the company believes it needs to manage the business over the planning horizon, determined on a true underlying economic basis and allowing for the planned future growth. This can differ from the regulatory capital requirement because regulatory capital requirements can be based on a company being closed to new business, derived using parameters or calculations prescribed by the regulator, and effectively not representative of the true underlying economics of the business as it would be viewed by management unfettered by regulation. Even regulatory frameworks that are based on economic principles can provide areas of difference as a result of

- the economic capital requirements reflecting the capital required to write new business over the planning horizon, a regulatory basis focussing on a closed business in run-off;
- different views of minimum financial strength targets, for example, a regulator may target a financial strength equivalent to 'BBB', or a company may require a higher rating to do business in a market as outlined previously for some general insurers and reinsurers;
- different views of economic parameters or drivers, such as illiquidity premium, for example, a regulator is interested in whether the balance sheet can cover the costs associated with buying appropriate insurance products[9] (hedges and reinsurance), rather than just the underlying evolution of actual market experience;
- regulations may have areas of prescription about how to allow for potential obligations to investors and how their capital can be assumed to be used that may differ from an internal view;
- different views on the cost of capital, for example, the regulator establishing a cost of capital based on a company being in different financial circumstances than the current operating levels.

An organisation needs to form its own view of the amount of capital it believes it needs to hold to meet its strategic objectives on a realistic economic basis.[10]

4.3.3.5   Peer benchmarks

These provide a valuable insight into the expectations generated by the market in which the company operates. Stakeholders do not want to see the company perform out of line with its peers in significant adverse events. Hence, understanding the dynamics of your capital position relative to that of peers is crucial. As the amount of capital that is established as an economic target will have implications for the overall risk-adjusted return, it is important to understand the size of this capital target relative to that of your peers in order to ensure that the drag that the buffer will create on performance is not too dissimilar.

Presently in the market, companies that hold higher economic capital buffers are typically players that target a higher level of financial strength as part of their business proposition, for example, reinsurers for which it can be a prerequisite of being a market participant.

Those businesses with smaller capital buffers tend to be those that do not benefit greatly from diversification[11] or that have relatively stable financial positions. For many of these market participants, the cost of capital required to compete would be too high if the buffer were larger.

The use of peer group comparators needs to consider each company's ability (and willingness) to access additional sources of capital. Some companies may have extreme ratios of debt to equity, or not be willing to access certain capital markets, as in the case of mutual companies that may not want to demutualise by raising equity. A company's access to capital or its willingness to raise certain forms of capital may influence a Board's view of the size of the buffer that they wish to carry.

Finally, each company will determine its financial position by taking account of its ability to take management actions under circumstances in which there might be a high risk of breaching regulatory capital requirements. Actions that have been incorporated into the models and which form part of the assessment of the current financial position will not be available to restore a financial position should it deteriorate. Rather, they must be taken as determined in order to maintain the currently reported financial position. Only actions that have not been included in the financial calculations to date can restore a financial position to the target level, should the position move outside a tolerable bound. Thus, the number of actions available that have not been incorporated within the financial modelling will provide a sense of the financial flexibility of the company. It should be noted that each company within a peer group will have a different number of these actions available.

4.3.3.6   *Rating agency perspectives*

A rating agency awards a rating based on, among other things, its assessment of an organisation's solvency and ability to take action to manage the solvency position in reasonably adverse scenarios. Hence, different rating targets will affect the amount of capital a company has to hold. For example, if the Group targets a credit rating of A, this may correspond to a 1-in-1000 chance of becoming insolvent, based on default statistics from the corporate bond market where as a BBB rating may be based on a 1-in-200 chance of insolvency.

In some industry sectors, firms will only do business with organisations that have at least a certain financial strength rating, which means the rating agency view is important. The rating agency capital perspective is also important because it is one of the cornerstones of the rating process[12] from which the cost of raising capital is determined should the company need to go the market and raise more capital.

4.3.3.7   *Current and historical capital cover ratios*

The capital cover ratios for each year and the rolling averages over multiple periods can provide useful insight into the capital buffer implied by the approach to the management of the company over the last few years. It provides an important input to the process as it illustrates the actual behaviour of the organisation and the buffer with which the Board has actually felt comfortable, irrespective of the statements that have been made in disclosures.

4.3.3.8   *Industry practice*

Where there is a reasonable degree of consistency between the economic views underpinning the regulatory balance sheet and the company's own internal economic balance sheet, companies tend to prefer to express the economic capital requirement as a buffer over the regulatory capital requirement. This is because this approach reduces the number of calculations and metrics that need to be monitored and makes it easier to explain to analysts.

Where such an approach is used, care must be taken to ensure that the different dynamics between the economic and regulatory bases are understood. Usually, recalculation triggers are established so that, should events occur that cause the capital requirements to move in different ways, thereby changing the size of the required economic capital buffer, the models will be rerun and the capital risk appetite buffer re-assessed.

An area that requires careful consideration is the inclusion or exclusion of management actions within the basis of the calculation. It is possible that some actions can only be triggered once the business has taken the decision to close to new business. This means that, while these actions may be appropriate for inclusion in the regulatory assessment of capital, they may not be appropriate for inclusion in the projection of the economic capital position and the assessment of the capital available to grow the business after adverse events have occurred.

Within the insurance sector, common capital adequacy risk appetite statements are:

> *We will hold a sufficient capital buffer at Group level to ensure that we only breach the regulatory capital requirements in a 1-in-X-year event.*
>
> *We target a S&P/Moody's rating of 'XXX' on our senior debt, at all times staying above 'YYY'.*

The most common probability of breaching regulatory capital requirements is at the 1-in-10-year level. There is an additional clustering of companies that target around a 1-in-25-year event. These clusterings would appear to align with key credit rating grades.

4.3.4   Second risk appetite dimension – earnings

4.3.4.1   Approach for calibrating the earnings risk appetite statement

The profits of an organisation build the financial strength of the balance sheet and provide the funds to invest in developing the business. Once a company has done this, any residual profits form the basis on which it makes distributions to shareholders and other interested parties. Shareholders would like to see some element of stability in this profit stream to provide some comfort and assurity over the likely level of the dividends. The profits that are declared will also form the media headline that creates the public opinion on whether the management of the organisation are receiving fair reward for what they have delivered.

As there are many balance sheets that are reported to various stakeholders, there are a multitude of potentially different definitions of 'profitability'. Within any single balance sheet, depending on the items included, it is also possible to develop different profit measures. For example, it is possible to find the following incarnations in Report and Accounts – operating profit, underlying profit and bottom line profit.

It is essential for a company to understand which measures of profit are important to stakeholders. The profitability from the core business proposition is a useful starting point as this is usually the profit that management feel most able to influence and control. The vagaries of financial markets and the performance of company pension funds are aspects some managers believe are outside their direct control. With this in mind, it is useful for a company to look back to the business model statements and develop a definition that enables the stakeholders to see what profit has been made from the activities that underlie the business model.

In developing the dimension for the risk appetite, there is little additional value to developing a measure for earnings that is identical to the movement in the level of the balance sheet used in the capital risk appetite statement as this will add little additional insight. If the movement is identical, the likelihood is that the actions to manage the capital and earnings risk appetite statements have equivalent impacts, and thus, one of the statements may not add to the decision-making process.

One of the key attributes to extracting value from a risk appetite framework is ensuring that senior management buy-in and are remunerated according to the variability of performance of the metrics. Aligning remuneration encourages them to pay close attention to managing the metrics. In order to achieve this, management need to feel that the definition of the earnings risk appetite dimension is one that incorporates elements over which they can exert control.

In calibrating this risk appetite dimension, multiple inputs can be used to gain both market and internal perspectives, including

– peer benchmarks,
– actual and planned historical own-company earnings experience,
– the company's planned and stressed levels of future earnings,
– levels at which profit warnings and dividend cuts would become a material concern.

The following sections discuss these perspectives.

4.3.4.2 *Peer benchmarks*

Analysis of how peers have actually performed over the past few years and the relative movements in share prices when announcements have been made that differ from those expected can provide a sense of market expectations.

4.3.4.3 *Historical own-company earnings experience*

The company's own actual and planned earnings figures provide an insight into the historical volatility of the different profit and loss lines and how they have deviated from the plan. The use of historical experience also helps the company calibrate the risk appetite statement so that it provides a sensible and reasonable target given the current position of the company. Evidencing that delivering performance objectives within these bounds will ensure management buy-in is easier to achieve.

For example, if the earnings have always been extremely volatile, it will be difficult to get management to buy into applying a constraint that immediately changes this significantly and having their performance measured by remaining within a tight bound. The outcome from forcing such a calibration through could be an adverse change in behaviours and results being manipulated.

4.3.4.4   Company's planned and stressed future earnings

Risk appetite statements are forward looking, and thus, we are looking to establish statements for the future planning horizon. Understanding the company's planned and stressed levels of future earnings enables the calibration to be fitted to the company's position going forward, which will include the impact of the evolution of a changing risk profile.

4.3.4.5   Industry practice

As expressed at the outset, the earnings statement is critical to creating perceptions not only internally but also with external stakeholders. Thus, a company will want to ensure that the earnings are sufficiently stable to manage these expectations, including providing shareholders with a reasonably stable growing dividend.

Generally, the risk appetite statement focuses on monitoring one earnings measure, which is usually driven by the International Financial Reporting Standards (IFRS)[13] result. This is sensible, as the IFRS result is important to the financial disclosures and is the basis for declaring shareholder dividends. The most common profit measure is the operating profit. This captures all key operating effects, and is in line with IFRS accounting standards. The measure does introduce some elements of volatility which some observers suggest are not necessarily fully within the control of the business unit management team, such as Group centre costs. However, others argue that the key items should be reasonably within the control of a well-managed company and incentivise a holistic rather than a siloed approach to the management of the business and delivery of its strategy.

The following statements are examples of those used within the industry:

The Group's operating profit over the next 12 months must be X per cent of planned operating profit in a 1-in-X-year event.

We will not miss our consensus earnings forecast by more than X per cent at a Y per cent confidence level.

We will aim consistently to target a dividend of XXX.

The majority of companies appear to target an operating profit of at least £0 after a 1-in-10-year event.

4.3.5   Third risk appetite dimension – liquidity

4.3.5.1   Approach for calibrating the liquidity risk appetite statement

With lack of liquidity to pay stakeholders when they are due sealing the demise of many financial institutions, it is not surprising to find liquidity as a key focus for organisations. As well as being able to meet cash flow demands under normal day-to-day conditions, the financial crisis high-lighted the need to be able to do this under reasonably extreme scenarios in which a number of adverse events come together, for example:

– a downturn in financial markets,
– an increase in demand from depositors for their cash to be withdrawn from institutions they believed were not financially secure, coupled with
– cash flow demands from collateral calls and
– the need to resolve credit lines in markets that had seized.

The cash flow requirements include payments of claims to customers, staff salaries, collateral calls on derivatives, coupons and redemption proceeds to debtholders, and dividends to shareholders. The high risk of not being able to meet cash flow requirements has resulted in many banks being forced into state ownership.

Many cash flow assessments rely on output from models developed for financial reporting purposes. These models have not necessarily been established to identify all cash flow demands in various scenarios, such as collateral movements or the timing of debt refinancing, which could lead to an imprudent assessment of the liquidity needs in adverse circumstances. Management should be clear on questioning which cash flows have been included and thinking about the sort of cash or asset calls that could arise.

In undertaking the calibration of the liquidity risk appetite statement, multiple inputs can be used to gain both market and internal perspectives, including

– peer benchmarks,
– actual and planned historical company cash flow information

– planned future cash flows and stressed future cash flows
– frequency with which calculations are re-assessed

The following sections expand on these inputs.

4.3.5.2   Peer benchmarking

The use of peer benchmarking provides a reasonableness check on the extent of liquid asset coverage requirements being specified. This ensures that

– the base investment return drag that may arise as a result of holding liquid assets is not out of line with peers;
– the events that may give rise to damage to the organisation's reputation as a result of liquidity issues are not out of line with peers.

4.3.5.3   Historical own-company experience

The company's own historical experience can be used to inform the nature of adverse events that have arisen, which can provide perspective to the calibration of the stressed scenarios and whether the cash flow projections from the organisation's modelling provide reasonable estimates of the cash flows that may arise.

4.3.5.4   Industry practice

Common liquidity risk appetite statements are

> *Across the Group, we must meet our business-as-usual net cash outflows on a day-to-day basis.*
>
> *Across the Group, we must have sufficient liquid assets to appropriately cover the net cash outflows over the next 12 months after a 1-in-X event.*

The two statements cover the need to maintain sufficient liquidity to meet net cash outflows on a day-to-day basis as well as after a reasonably extreme adverse event has occurred.

It is important to be able to meet these cash flow requirements without needing to sell assets at a significant discount (known as a 'fire sale' or valued with a significant haircut) or in a way that moves the market pricing materially.

From market information up to 2012, the predominant stressed liquidity event was equivalent to a 1-in-10-year event.

While many companies assess the ability to meet the liquidity requirements in the following 12 months, it is important to understand the impact on the profile of 'cash liquidity' over the coming years. This is because the result of the risk appetite assessment may be that it is possible following a significant adverse event to meet cash flows this year; however, the actions to do so may have implications for meeting cash flows in subsequent years. For example, the company may have debt due for repayment in the coming few years that either relies on liquidity that has now been used to meet more immediate demands under the adverse scenario or is difficult to refinance because of adverse credit markets. Effectively, this is about understanding the wider implications of any actions taken under adverse conditions to meet immediate liquidity requirements.

Additionally, some companies look at cash flows over the coming 24 months rather than just 12 months. Partly, this is because of the frequency with which the calculations are performed. For example, if the assessment is undertaken annually, it may be that the assessment misses the refinancing risk associated with an event 18 months into the future.

4.3.5.5 *Liquidity stress defined scenarios*

In determining the stressed liquidity requirements, it is important to consider the potential cash flow calls under a variety of scenarios. These scenarios should cover a variety of different extreme events in which the cash flow demands of various stakeholder groups are stressed, for example, scenarios in which

- customers make a significantly increased number of claims against the company, such as withdrawals from savings contracts or claims from catastrophic events;
- counterparties default to which the company has a significant aggregate exposure;
- banks make significant calls for collateral to be placed;
- investors have the ability to call for investments to be redeemed, or income payments to be made;
- the ability to refinance loans is limited or only achievable at a significantly increased cost.

4.3.5.6 *Liquid assets*

In order to assess the liquidity and value for which assets could be realised in these stressed conditions, a number of companies utilise the framework from within the credit rating agency models to assess the liquidity risk on assets. This approach has the benefits, from the company's perspective, of being objective and aligned with the information provided to credit rating agencies for credit rating assessment purposes.

4.3.6   Fourth risk appetite dimension – franchise value

4.3.6.1   Approach to the calibration of the franchise value dimension

The franchise value dimension encapsulates the desire to build and sustain a business in the medium- to long term. Shareholders and management want to grow the business to increase reward through dividends, appreciation in the value of investments, performance bonuses, and the ability to enhance service or the customer proposition. Thus, understanding the elements that could lead to a reduction in the franchise value is important to these stakeholder groups.

The strategic plan outlines how management believe they can develop the business over the next few years, including how they will manage the risks. Delivery of the plan requires an an articulation of the company's capacity to manage risk, which is about both its financial flexibility and its capability in terms of people, processes and systems. The franchise value risk appetite dimension covers the non-financial operational aspects of risk capacity such as reputation, legislation, people and knowledge, processes, systems and project stretch.

The franchise value dimension encapsulates

– how the organisation wants to be seen in terms of its brand and reputation with its key stakeholders in order to ensure people remain satisfied in wanting to do business with it or act as brand ambassadors, thus, sustaining the new business development capability, and
– ensures the business plan, which underpins the belief in the organisation, is delivered and delivered appropriately.

A franchise value risk appetite statement is outlined below:

We will seek to uphold our brand and reputation with customers, staff and other external parties, and ensure we deliver what we say we will in a manner appropriate to our values and beliefs.

Common considerations within the franchise value risk appetite dimension are

1. customers and distribution – customer retention and distribution are key drivers of ensuring the franchise is maintained into the future. This

requires companies to be delivering on promises and with an appropriate level of service quality. This can also be extended to provide a view as to whether the products are designed in a way that is meeting the customer needs.

2. capital markets – an adverse view of the organisation from its capital markets would give rise to a potentially higher cost of capital, reduced profitability or the ability to write new business. These could result in damage to the franchise value.

3. media and public – the media and public perception can impact the willingness of
   - customers to buy products and services from a company,
   - customers who have already bought products to remain with the company,
   - investors to provide capital, and
   - the willingness of high-quality staff to work for and remain with the company.

   These issues can all lead to damage of the franchise value.

4. regulation and legislation – Material breaches of either regulation or legislation would have a significant impact on the franchise value. The regulator could levy significant fines, restrict an organisation's license to write new business, and require an organisation to expend money to rectify a situation at a speed that increases cost and redirects staff from other tasks.

5. third-party suppliers – outsourcing activities to a third party can give rise to brand and reputational damage if these third parties behave in a manner that is not in keeping with the company's standards. The media might connect the company name with any issues arising within the operations of a third-party supplier, and external stakeholders tend to hold the company responsible for resolving the issues for the third party.

6. operational delivery – a company needs to deliver the plan that has been developed on paper. The ability to deliver the plan on an ongoing basis increases the belief of analysts and rating agencies in the management team's ability to deliver on what they say they can. This credibility and trust are also based on the quality of the analysis and projections that form the basis of the information on which the business is managed. Ensuring the information and infrastructure are suited to this purpose assists in building a good reputation.

Table 4.2 provides a summary of the various groups outlined above and metrics that could be used to monitor drivers of their perceptions that could

Table 4.2 Summary of potential metrics for the franchise value risk appetite dimension

Stakeholder group	Purpose and objective	Metrics
Customers and	Ensure customers will be satisfied with our products and overall approach to doing business	New customer volumes Existing customer retention Customer satisfaction Customer engagement Customer service levels First contact resolution rate Customer complaints Customer proposition hot spots Ombudsman complaints
Distributors	Ensure our distribution partners are satisfied to continue doing business with us, our service is satisfactory, our products are competitively priced and a good value for customers	Distributor satisfaction Satisfying service level agreements
Capital markets	Ensure we meet rating agency and investor requirements and address their concerns	Credit rating and watch rating Analyst buy/hold signals Returns to participating members Changes in rating agency risk and capital model results
Public and media	Uphold our brand and reputation among the general public	Brand awareness Media coverage
Regulators	Ensure that regulator is happy that we are meeting their objectives for the market	Delivering on agreed plans for responding to regulator's issues Compliance report Audit findings

Policymakers	Ensure we lobby against those policies that are detrimental to the interest of our stakeholders	Engagement with industry bodies Engagement with policymakers
Third-party suppliers	Ensure those we do business with act in a way that will not damage our brand or reputation	Sanction checks Service level agreements Negative media coverage
Operational delivery	Ensure we can 'do what it says on the tin' and build credibility in the marketplace Understand how our staff perceive us as an employer, assess their belief in our products and values, and willingness to act as brand ambassadors	New business value add Staff advocacy, engagement or satisfaction scores Adverse leaver rate Pressure on living the company values Project schedule variance Project cost variance System error rates System run rates System down time Capacity utilisation rates
Competitors	Ensure we respond to prevent the actions of our competitors from doing damage to our new business capability or brand	Share of voice Competitor financial strength watch rating Innovation and new products

underpin the franchise risk appetite statement.[14] The following sections expand on the metrics for each group outlined in Table 4.2.

4.3.6.2   Customers and distributors dimension

The measures outlined in Table 4.2 track how satisfied customers and distributors are with the organisation. The purpose of the measures is to ensure that the organisation offers products and services that meet customers' needs and provide good value for the money. As it is important for the company to retain existing customers and avoid adverse publicity through poor customer experience, this dimension also monitors the quality of the customer experience after the purchase. Similarly, in the case of distributors, the company wants to ensure its products and services are such that distributors want to continue to do business with the company in the future and recommend it to their clients ahead of competitors.

Customer satisfaction and engagement.   Two measures of customer perception are the levels of new business being written and the ability to retain existing customers. A significant number of customers will not complain, but rather 'vote with their feet'. Therefore, monitoring take-up rates and retention rates against planned levels will provide an indication of customer satisfaction.

Many companies carry out a customer satisfaction survey. An alternative measure is customer engagement, which only measures those customers whose survey responses are 'completely satisfied'. The indicator was the result of research by Xerox in the 1990s that suggested that even customers who were satisfied were still significantly likely to defect to competitors. Thus, some organisations prefer to monitor customer engagement, or loyalty, particularly where they service a specialist client base, such as a profession in which the provision of products and services from another source is possible and would be significantly detrimental to the business model.

First-contact resolution rate.   The ability of a company to deal with queries from customers in their first contact can provide an indication of whether customers are satisfied with the solution the company provides. A customer whose query takes a while to resolve may become disengaged and choose to take his or her business elsewhere. It may be more appropriate to monitor the number of contacts before resolution or the time to resolution. If automated systems are used to monitor these dimensions, there is a risk that the system may be gamed in order to manage the automated monitoring information, and queries may be closed before customers are satisfied with the resolution. This would be something that needs to be independently checked from time to time.

Customer proposition hot spots.   The 'customer proposition hot spots' score aggregates results from how an organisation manages its approach and delivery to customers. It covers areas such as the appropriateness of product design, ability to provide information that is clear and concise, the quality of any advice, quality of service, and the ease with which the customer can do business with the company.

Monitoring complaints.   Monitoring the number of customer complaints provides an objective and readily available measure of customer dissatisfaction with aspect of a company's business.

In the United Kingdom, the Financial Ombudsman Service (FOS) acts as an official independent expert in settling complaints between consumers and businesses providing financial services. The actual number of FOS complaints, the number of complaints upheld and the increase in the number of complaints can be used to monitor customer dissatisfaction that could lead to brand damage.

Distribution partner satisfaction.   Distribution partners' perceptions of the company, its products and its service standards can be collected using simple questionnaires, which can be monitored on a regular basis to understand the level of distribution partner satisfaction with the company living up to its expectations. Dissatisfied distributors could result in declining volumes of new business being written through certain channels.

4.3.6.3   *Capital markets dimension*

This stakeholder group has a significant influence over the willingness of people to invest in the organisation, the cost of raising capital and the perceived value of the capital held by the organisation. The objective of the metric is to monitor whether the company is meeting rating agency and investor expectations and dealing with their concerns efficiently and effectively.

Credit rating agencies.   The view of credit rating agencies can be monitored using a financial strength and watch-rating metric.

Rating agencies publish their current and future views of an organisation's financial strength through the rating agency financial strength rating and the watch rating respectively.

Investment analysts.   Investment analysts provide views on whether the shares of an organisation should be bought, sold or held. This, in addition to some general market related information, provides insight into the market's perception of a company. Information is monitored from a consistent short-list of investment analysts. In addition, relative trading volumes, volume of trading by directors, and the performance of the stock relative to a peer group can be used to enhance the measure.

Participating members.   For some organisations, this policyholder group has been a provider of capital. This capital has been supplied with the expectation of some reward in return. The metrics for this dimension will vary greatly depending on the nature of the contract established with the stakeholder group. The aspects may cover dimensions such as investment return, ratios of expenses to annual premium levels, levels of projected expense inflation, and the likelihood of allocations of additional bonus or miscellaneous surplus.

4.3.6.4   Public and media

This metric tracks the perception of the company's brand. A good brand image may influence new customers to choose products and services from the company rather than competitors.

For example, Ratners was a successful British jewellery company, led by Gerald Ratner. In April 1991, Gerald Ratner gave a speech to the Institute of Directors in which he joked about the quality of the products his company offered being poor. The jokes got laughs from the audience. However, the newspapers interpreted the remarks as making fun of his customers and the bad publicity that followed smashed his near £1bn turnover overnight. Ratner's market value plummeted at the same time, resulting in the firm's collapse. These events were damaging not only for the company, but they also ended Gerald Ratner's tenure as chief executive of the company his father had founded.

Brand awareness.   Awareness of the brand can be collated from prompted feedback from the public, analysed by subgroups that the company aims to target with its products or services. Many external providers collate information on behalf of companies and provide feedback to support this measure.

Media coverage.   Monitoring the proportion of negative company coverage across all types of media captures the aspects that could lead to brand damage. Analysing the data by the source of the coverage (television, newspapers, Twitter and so forth) enables the company to target response plans at the source of any potential damage. Again, many external providers collate information on behalf of companies and provide feedback to support this measure.

4.3.6.5 Regulators

Generally, a company does not aim to have significant regulatory or legislative breaches such that their reputation may be damaged by public disclosure of failures and fines, or their authorisation to do business being revoked. As part of being 'in business', it is necessary for an organisation to accept that it may need to tolerate some minor regulatory issues, although major breaches will not be tolerated.

Many of the recent regulatory issues have arisen as a result of the mis-selling of products, illegal practices and significant financial misstatements. These are difficult issues for which to provide forward-looking measures without inadvertently causing increased regulatory concern. A solution is to create 'hot spot' metrics that ensure the business actively monitors high-risk areas. For example, a business can

- use the underlying risk drivers of mis-selling issues of the past to develop a matrix for rating various products (for example, product complexity, target market sophistication, and so forth). The rating from this process is notched down if the product has been reviewed by audit and compliance within the last one to two years. This strategy incentivises a regular review process to check for changes in information or attitudes.
- assess the proportion of the premium that relates to the expected cost of claims from customers. If the proportion of the premium that relates to customer claims is small, there is a high risk that the product is not appropriate nor fair value for customers. For example, consider a premium of £100 that is made up of £60 for expenses and commission, £10 for tax, £20 for profit and £10 to cover the cost of claims from customers.

Similar approaches to monitoring hot spots can be taken for other issues such as material weaknesses in the external financial reporting process, in which metrics such as the number of uncorrected misstatements are monitored.

As companies aim to ensure that they are addressing regulatory concerns in a prompt and efficient way, a number of them monitor progress on actions they have agreed upon with regulators in response to issues raised during regulatory assessment and review processes.

4.3.6.6   Policymakers

A company actively engaging policymakers on issues that are in the interest of its stakeholders supports the alignment of the company's objectives with those of its stakeholders.

Measures that track this engagement include the provision of responses to key issues, the active membership of key industry bodies and engagement with policymakers.

4.3.6.7   Third-party suppliers

In many decisions to outsource arrangements to third parties, consideration is focussed on the cost-benefit analysis. with less thought given to the risks associated with brand and reputation. In the eyes of the public and external stakeholders, the company's name will be connected with any issues that arise, whether it blames the supplier for failing to meet standards or not. The public tend also to hold the company accountable for resolving the issues effectively. Consider these situations:

– Matalan and Primark brands outsourced services to a factory in Bangladesh. In 2013, their brands appeared in the media following the collapse of the factory building, allegedly resulting from negligence in maintaining a standard of health and safety. Matalan and Primark pledged financial support for the victims of the disaster.
– Lululemon recalled a large proportion of its 'yoga pants' because a material defect made them rather revealing. Lululemon blamed their supplier, but the incident cost them millions of dollars in revenue.

Service agreements need to include provisions for transfers of information relating to how the supplier is meeting the standards required by the company, including compliance with company standards, and the speed with which issues are resolved. Contracts should ensure that the company is able to review the supplier on-site regularly. Effectively, the supplier should be viewed as an extension of the organisation and subject to the same standards of quality, compliance and behaviour.

4.3.6.8   Operational delivery

The business plan exists as a theoretical exercise unless it is delivered. It is important that companies establish metrics to monitor the risks to the delivery of the plan and also the manner in which it is being delivered – that companies are 'living their values'.

New business value add.   A key element of franchise value and the strategic plan is the assessment of the potential value added from writing new business. This metric assesses whether the plan remains on target. Assessing this element in a similar way to supermarkets, that is, looking at 'like for like' sales, removes distortions from bringing on new products, brokers or distribution channels and can indicate whether the growth in new areas is damaging the service or attention being given to the existing distribution channels.

System and process quality.   The pressure placed on systems and processes as a company grows can lead to deterioration in quality and potentially unfortunate adverse publicity. In 2012, issues with systems led to reputational damage for banks when customers were unable to access their accounts.

It is difficult to create 'lead' indicators to assess the likelihood of such a major event happening, but it is possible to determine whether there are a significant number of more minor outages or errors on key systems that may lead to customer dissatisfaction or delivery issues. The metric could include

– cumulative IT down time and number of incidents
– error or system failure rates
– capacity utilisation rates
– delivery to agreed service standards

Employee stakeholder group.   An organisation wants its employees to be willing to sell the company to other employees and external parties. The company can create the passion to do this by

- living the values and creating a good working environment,
- managing internal talent and opportunities for career progression,
- managing resources so that staff are not overstretched to deliver a plan or set unrealistic targets.

The manifestation of these issues is seen through an impact on staff morale and turnover rates, which if adversely impacted, could make it increasingly difficult to deliver the business plan within budget.

Two metrics that track the employee stakeholder group are an adverse leaver rate and staff survey results.

Adverse leaver rate.   If employees leave an organisation for reasons that suggest they would not be a positive advocate for the company, there is a risk that their views, expressed in the market, could damage the reputation of the company in the longer term, making it more difficult to attract customers and quality staff. The organisation can monitor the total number of leavers over the previous 12 months who departed for negative reasons divided by the total number of current full-time employees. 'Negative reasons' for leaving are those driven by the employee's dissatisfaction with the organisation or its management, such as unreasonable targets, insufficient career opportunities, and the culture and the job being different from what was described at the interview. Companies collate the data using a simple exit survey to monitor a list of reasons why staff choose to leave.

Staff advocacy, engagement or satisfaction scores.   Staff engagement and satisfaction are defined in the same way as for customer engagement and satisfaction. Staff advocacy is an alternative presentation of the engagement score, which consists of a figure that is the number of very satisfied staff less the number of very dissatisfied staff. Many organisations conduct an annual staff survey to measure employee satisfaction, coupled with 'flash' mini-surveys throughout the year. These surveys can be provided by external consultants who can also benchmark the results against a peer group. However, the staff survey results may provide a false reading depending on the reasons why people are leaving. If people who exit are on average negative about the company, it may highlight an issue and a talent drain that is key to delivery of the plan. As a result, monitoring both the adverse leaver rate and staff advocacy measures may enable the company to identify the issue.

Pressure on living the company values.   The company values are central to the organisational culture and to ensuring that activities are not undertaken that put the brand at heightened risk. If we are cutting corners on behaving in line with our values to meet operational delivery requirements, there are numerous potential adverse outcomes, including inappropriate implementation of infrastructure solutions, loss of talented staff, hindrance of operational delivery, communications that mislead investors, cognisant misstatement of financial accounts, breakdown in business dynamics, and court cases related to harassment and bullying.

The metric is constructed from views expressed in staff exit interviews, feedback from the 'culture and values' subsection of the employee engagement survey, and evidence that the organisation considers its values when making decisions.

Project delivery dimension.   Many plans are developed with a requirement to deliver a number of projects at the same time. During the year, there is usually additional unplanned work that can lead to key resources being overstretched and result in projects not being delivered to time, or budgeted spend escalating excessively.

For each project, measuring the variance relative to the agreed project schedule and budget can provide insight into the stretch and risk to the delivery of the business plan. These can be presented as

- variance to plan – the difference between the planned completion time and the actual completion time;
- variance to budget – the difference between the planned budget and the actual spend.

Other measures that are used cover aspects such as the number of inflight projects, total project spend, the number of projects per sponsor and the proportion of key staff members' time allocated to project work, the number of contractor staff being utilised.

In identifying the key staff members, it should be borne in mind that it is rarely the executives who are stretched in this regard, but that there are key resource pinchpoints within teams that are pulled in all directions as each executive attempts to deliver his or her own projects that compete for the same operational resources.

5
Stress and Scenario Testing

This chapter provides coverage of the role of stress and scenario testing, a key element in the tool kit of the risk function. In particular, it will

– define the various approaches to stress and scenario testing and illustrate how they can be used;
– explain how to develop scenarios in a way that enables value to be extracted from the output;
– illustrate how stress and scenario testing can be used to identify opportunities.

5.1 Questions for the Board

Stress and scenario testing (SST) is a key part of the toolbox of the chief risk officer. Stress and scenario testing can be used to help the Board understand

1. how management has evidenced that it understands the risks they are running in delivering the plan and how to manage them;
   – what the triggers are for the strategy or plan to be reviewed;
2. where the business model is vulnerable and what can be done to reduce that vulnerability;
   – what events could mean that the objectives are not being delivered or risk appetites being breached, and what actions could mitigate the extent of the impact;
   – at what point the market could lose confidence in the company, and how the company would react;
   – when the company might no longer be able to carry out its business activities;

3. how it knows that the risk appetite will guide the delivery of the company's objectives and limits are actively constraining excessive deviation from plan;
4. how it knows how much authority has been delegated to the executive team to deliver the plan on a day-to-day basis without referral to the Board;
5. the range of potential future economic scenarios (for example, those used to develop the equity stress test), where historic events would be represented;
6. the implications of making an estimation error in the assessment of various extreme events or key assumptions in new business pricing;
7. the sensitivity of the risks and rewards from target markets;
8. the convexity of the company's risk exposures, that is, how does the size of the exposure change as the position or level of the financial markets changes?

5.2 What is stress and scenario testing?

SST has evolved along a similar path to that of risk management. Generally, it is used as a defensive tool to identify actions to protect the business from material losses resulting from adverse events. Over time, we will see SST evolving into a more strategic tool that aims to draw out the threats and opportunities associated with alternative outcomes, within which actions are identified to determine how to manage the adverse outcomes and position the business to take advantage of potential opportunities.

Historically, business plans were presented as a single target projection with little work done to understand the uncertainties that existed in the potential projected outcome. Over time, companies have started to introduce sensitivities to this 'central planning scenario' as a way of providing some understanding of the potential outturn if things do not go exactly as planned or key assumptions were set incorrectly. For example, projections may have assumed a return of 5 per cent p.a. in each of the next five years; simple and pragmatic as an assumption this may be, it is important to understand what happen and how would we respond to manage the business if we had a sudden economic dip?

If we look back over the last few years, who would have imagined we would witness the following situations:

1. The credit crisis was derived from a build-up of extremely large notional amounts on what was thought to be very low probability of the loss super-

senior tranches of collateralised debt obligations (CDOs). Few understood the shortcomings of the models and what would happen if the lack of relevant data for setting the assumptions resulted in a significant under-estimation of the risks.

2. International airspace was shut down for two weeks, and holidaymakers were stranded because of volcanic ash in Iceland.

In some industries the notion of testing things and testing to destruction is more common practice. For example, ballistics testing of armoured vehicles and the fatigue testing of materials and structures is commonplace in the engineering field. The concept in financial services is in a process of evolution.

Over the years, the use of 'what if...?' scenarios in financial services companies has widened to cover all areas of an organisation. Presently, areas that most benefit from the use of SST are

(a) strategic planning
(b) setting risk appetite, tolerances and limits
(c) risk monitoring and management information, including information for capital planning such as testing capital requirements from scenarios around the level prescribed for regulatory purposes, or to assess the convexity of capital requirements as actual outcomes fluctuate around the level assumed
(d) pricing and product development
(e) new initiatives, including merger and acquisition activity
(f) performance and incentive planning
(g) testing and validating the business operating model
(h) testing responses to technological threats, such as cyber attacks

Table 5.1 summarises inputs and uses of stress and scenario testing.

5.3 Types of stress and scenario testing

In general, there are three types of assessment:

1. single-factor stress testing – flexing a single parameter to an extreme but plausible extent[1].
2. scenario testing – a forward-looking assessment of changes in a combination of factors.
3. reverse scenario testing (RST) – an iterative process to identify the type and severity of an event or combination of events which could cause

Table 5.1 Summary of inputs and uses of stress and scenario testing

Inputs	Assessment framework	Uses

– Business plans
– The Group's risk profile
– Business Unit risk profile
– Product risk profile
– Emerging risk profile
– Strategic risk profile
– CRO's top ten risk list
– Board and management input from workshops
– Historical events
– Historical company performance/experience
– Commentary from market participants about the future outlook
– Expert judgment
– Current and future political, economic, social, technological, legislative, environmental and regulatory position
	1. Single-factor tests
	  – Realistic stresses aligned with setting and testing the risk appetite and limits
	  – Key assumption sensitivities, particularly where direct-experience data is sparse
	  – Product line stresses
	  – Validation and testing of a model or proposal
	
	2. Scenario tests
	  – Base
	  – Market forecast
	  – Historical events rolled forward to apply in current environment
	  – Past company performance/experience
	  – Synthetically constructed scenarios
	
	3. Reverse scenario tests
	  – Assessment of causes of failure to achieve objectives
	  – Assessment of causes of breaches to risk appetite and tolerances
	  – Assessment of causes of failure to meet stakeholder expectations
		– Business planning process to evidence management understands the risks in the plan and how to manage them.
		– Identify business model vulnerabilities, take actions to reduce vulnerabilities or develop contingency plans
		– Put the risk appetite and limits in context and understand the level of responsibility that has been delegated
		– Understand the key assumptions in product pricing and profitability
		– Provide information for capital planning and assessment of initiatives.
		– Understand when the performance incentive plan pays out
		– Test and validate the business operating model and operational frameworks

the business model of the organisation to fail. Effectively, this is about defining the outcome and backsolving to determine the potential causes.

5.3.1   Single-factor stress testing

Undertaking a number of these tests provides a standardised comparison of risk exposures, an understanding of how these exposures may change over time, and the sorts of events that may result in breaches to risk tolerances or limits. This information can then be used to develop appropriate management actions to mitigate individual risks.

5.3.2   Scenario testing

Scenario analysis can be developed from a number of information sources.

5.3.2.1   Historic experience

Applying expert judgment to rebase historic scenarios or experience such that it is relevant for 'today's environment' can be a very useful way of providing insight. The use of historical events enables management to put the impact of the events into a context that they may have experienced and find easier to understand than a mathematical expression such as 'this is a 1-in-100-year event....'

Applying expert judgment to historic events to make them relevant to the current environment requires an understanding of the backdrop to the event. For example, there may be evolutions of the financial markets, approaches to regulation or operation of the market that mean the evolution of the event will be different in the current environment for which judgment and adjustment need to be applied.

An additional advantage of historic events is that data will exist on the wider implications of events that have occurred, and the impacts in the years following the event as the markets readjust, which can be factored into the analysis. For example,

– many pandemics have wider financial market implications.
– the 2008 credit crisis resulted in changes in patterns of consumer spending and long-term rates of economic recovery.

5.3.2.2   Company-specific scenarios

Company-specific scenarios are particularly useful in cases in which the organisation has experience of more unique events as a result of its particular history, products or challenges. These can ensure that scenarios are tailored to the specific business, which can lead to better management buy-in and insight.

5.3.2.3 *Synthetically constructed scenarios*

Synthetically constructed scenarios are created from expert views of the potential evolution of events from the current situation. As these scenarios are not based on objective historic experience but expert judgment, these can be more difficult events for which to obtain management buy-in. However, they can capture the evolution of extreme events that may be missing from historic data or ones that would not have happened in the past, but the combination of current issues would give rise to these new threats.

For example, the evolution of 'tweeting' and instant messaging can give rise to immediate and more direct feedback that is shared across a global customer base in a manner over which the company has less control. The impact and speed of response required to mitigate negative comments, and the development of scenarios to help understand how a 'twitter' marketing campaign is managed would not have been supported by historical experience a few years ago.

In 2012, Waitrose, a UK supermarket chain with an upmarket image and largely middle-class customer base, tried to embrace the influence of Twitter by launching a promotional campaign. The campaign asked people to finish the sentence 'I shop at Waitrose because....'

Instead of receiving wholly positive tweets on which to build its global brand, Waitrose found itself subject to British humour, including responses such as 'I shop at Waitrose because I don't like being surrounded by poor people' and 'Do I shop at Waitrose? Don't be silly, I've got servants who do that for me'.

While it is not clear whether the campaign was a public relations disaster, it is doubtful that this turn of events featured in boardroom considerations prior to approving the campaign.

5.3.3 Reverse scenario testing (RST)

In the early years, as scenario testing became part of boardroom discussions, much of the discussion was about the likelihood of an event arising. Being precise with the level of likelihood of an event arising is less valuable than understanding the implications and actions for managing the implications should an event arise. This was the catalyst for RST, which approaches the analysis of scenarios from the opposite perspective – it defines the break point as the position at which the business model fails[2] and works backwards to define the scenario that would give rise to it.

RST is designed to focus debate on building an understanding of the circumstances under which the business model will fail, and consider the actions the company would take in these scenarios. The aim is to improve the understanding of the risks to the business model and ensure contingency plans exist to manage these key events should they arise, removing the emphasis from the precision of the likelihood of an event occurring.

Business model failure can be defined as a combination of events that breaches a threshold established for one or more elements of the company's risk appetite.

The inclusion of the reference to elements of the risk appetite within the definition of 'business model failure' aims to ensure consideration is given to issues wider than just the impact on the capital position. As we align risk appetite with the management of the performance objectives of the business, the definition of business model failure also frames 'failure' in terms of the key strategic risks to the business, and thus should prove of use to the Board. The types of scenarios that may be considered include

- inability to deliver the competitive difference
- exhaustion of capital
- insufficient liquid resources to meet requirements as they fall due
- inability to pay dividends over an extended period
- inability to service debt
- market refusal to provide or renew financial support
- sustained losses or inability to meet financial/commercial targets
- inability to meet operational commitments
- severe reputational damage
- closure to new business

Stress and scenario testing should not focus solely on single extreme events but also consider challenges that can arise from a prolonged year-on-year straining of the company.

For example, in the early 2000s many assessments of natural catastrophe risk did not consider the impact of multiple smaller events occurring, but focused on the impact of a single large event. Recent combinations of events such as earthquakes, tsunamis and hurricanes have caused significant losses for insurers. If questions had been asked about the impact of multiple less severe events and their potential for being interlinked, some of these impacts might have been drawn out.

In March 2011, an earthquake of magnitude 9.0 struck Japan and triggered subsequent tsunami waves that reached heights of up to 40 metres. The tsunami caused nuclear accidents, including meltdowns at the Fukushima Nuclear Power Plant. The Bank of Japan offered ¥15 trillion (US$180 billion) to the banking system to normalise market conditions.

Some geophysicists believe the Japan earthquake and tsunami were also linked to the earthquakes that had occurred in New Zealand a few months earlier. In September 2010, an earthquake of magnitude 7.1 had struck the South Island of New Zealand. Aftershocks included one of magnitude 6.3, in February 2011, near Christchurch, New Zealand.

5.4   How do we extract value from stress and scenario testing?

The key to extracting value is getting buy-in through simply making the events plausible, what we do relevant for the user, and the response plans realistic. The following sections explore achieving each of these elements in turn.

5.4.1   Making events plausible

Obtaining buy-in for stress and scenario testing is about getting all parties involved in developing plausible alternative events for their parts of the business and communicating these in a manner that helps the Board understand the thought processes. Facilitating and guiding these activities in an effective way is an important part of risk management's function.

A Bayesian network approach has proven useful for facilitating discussions and developing scenarios. A simple Bayesian network is outlined in Figure 5.1.

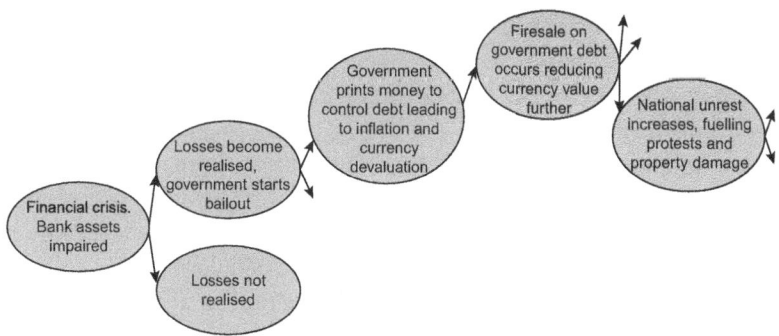

Figure 5.1   A Bayesian network

Figure 5.1 shows how the 'nodes' (bubbles) can help develop a story-board and set of alternative potential paths of the evolution of events. This approach helps identify the potential causal links (the order of the chain of events that leads to the end outcome), and thus the key risk drivers which the business needs to identify in order to monitor and determine appropriate actions should the events arise. Thus, a Bayesian network is a useful tool from which to build a storyboard for a scenario. As a method of achieving buy-in, providing a storyboard that enables experts to communicate scenarios and articulate the causal links is extremely valuable in helping the Board understand why a particular outcome is a plausible evolution of a series of events.

Allocating the nodes a likelihood of evolution (or probability of occurrence) also enables the company to develop a picture of plausible extreme events that can be used to validate risk and capital model output. The causal links can also be used to understand the drivers of interdependencies between risks, and thus, the appropriateness of the factors used to aggregate risk exposures together in the assessment of the capital requirements for the business (for example, correlation factors which can be used to adjust the result of the aggregation of the impacts of single stand-alone events, for the degree to which one event may be linked to another).

5.4.2   Making SST relevant

There are three areas that we find help make SST relevant.

First, we find that Boards and committees are 'switched off' when they receive a significant number of scenarios and action plans without any real context. Hence, it is important to have a filtering process to ensure that the Boards and committees are focusing on key scenarios relevant to the information being presented.

A large number of scenarios can arise as a result of engaging all the stakeholders in the business in developing multiple stress and scenario tests. In the process of engaging stakeholders, it is important to take their ideas seriously. Rejecting scenarios without giving the experts a feeling that their thoughts are being given fair consideration can result in them feeling disengaged from the process.

Therefore, it is necessary to develop a pragmatic approach to evaluating and filtering a large number of scenarios without it becoming a large, time-consuming calculation burden. The process must filter these ideas into the number of key scenarios to take forward for more detailed analysis and eventual presentation. Appendix C provides an example of a quick and simple way of filtering the ideas to ensure that the process that it is supporting does not grind to a halt.

Second, to assist in understanding why proposals are relevant, it is important to articulate the purpose for which the scenarios are being presented. This helps the users put the scenario and its implications in context.

Third, the manner of presentation needs to be considered. Expressing scenarios in a mathematical way limits the meaning to the users of the information. Telling a Board that a 1-in-10-year event could cost them £20m, and a 1-in-500-year event could cost £130m is unlikely to provide a basis from which to build an understanding of whether the event and outcome are reasonable, and the level of risk something with which the Board should feel comfortable. This is where a storyboard can help articulate why the evolution of the scenario is plausible and help the Board use their own experiences to assess reasonableness.

5.4.3   Making the response plans realistic

Having reached the point of successfully achieving buy-in for the scenarios, the value of the process is only extracted if response plans can be developed that are meaningful, proportionate and appropriate. We find that it is not the failure to identify risks but the failure to understand how to react that causes many companies to suffer material losses from events materialising.

The Board needs to understand that response plans are effectively asking them to sign-up to these actions being available to mitigate the impact from these risks that might arise. There is no value in having an action that states, for example, that the company will sell off a subsidiary to support its financial position if

- the sale is unlikely in that scenario because of a lack of buyers;
- the potential value the company attaches to the sale is unrealistic;
- when the company has to 'bite the bullet', it does not sell the entity because in reality it is a core business and the implications of doing so are much wider and greater, such as, for example, the company would close the entire organisation to new business as a result.

5.5   Looking for opportunities

As with risk management, the next evolution of stress and scenario analysis is to use the framework to identify opportunities as well as threats. Figure 5.2 shows a rather well-known turn of events that occurred over a period of years (somewhat now viewed as plausible).

In this example, with banks less able to originate loans, there is a market opportunity for others to provide a source of funding for a good return. Additionally, for those able to take advantage of the circumstances, there would be distressed assets available at fire sale prices. The use of stress and scenario analysis can help a company position itself to take advantage of such opportunities.

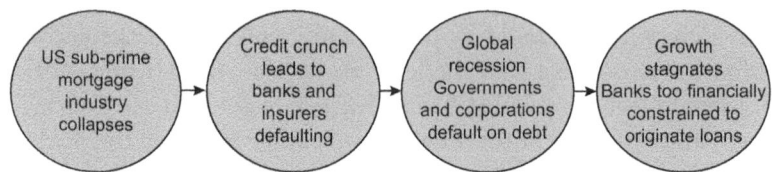

Figure 5.2   Evolution of a crisis and business opportunities

6
Operationalising the Management of Solvency and Capital

This chapter provides coverage of the operationalising of solvency and capital management. In particular, it will show

- how a Group can optimise capital fungibility through solvency management;
- the considerations for allocating economic capital to business units;
- the purpose and considerations in setting risk limits for a business unit.

The analysis within this section assumes that the Group structure consists of a Group centre ('Group') and three separate legal entities (SBU1, SBU2, SBU3), as outlined in Figure 6.1.

6.1 Operationalising solvency management

Generally, the solvency of an entity is reported using a solvency ratio and managed within an agreed solvency management corridor. This solvency management corridor is a set of ranges around a target solvency ratio usually represented as green, amber and red zones[1] as illustrated in Figure 6.2.

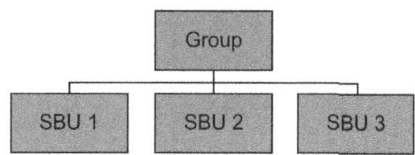

Figure 6.1 Assumed Group structure

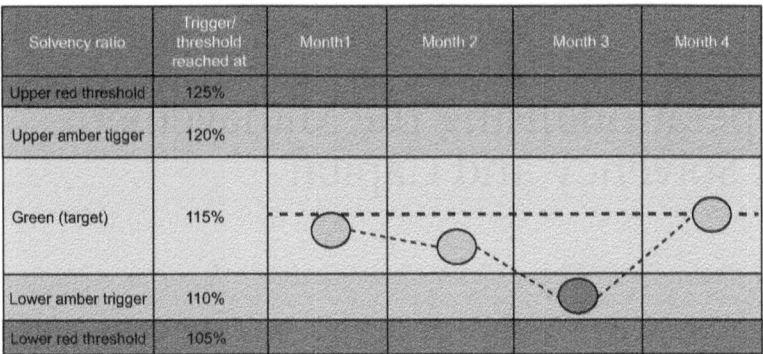

Solvency ratio	Trigger/ threshold reached at	Month 1	Month 2	Month 3	Month 4
Upper red threshold	125%				
Upper amber tigger	120%				
Green (target)	115%				
Lower amber trigger	110%				
Lower red threshold	105%				

Figure 6.2   Solvency management corridor

Solvency management is about being able to move financial resources or risks around the Group to ensure that all legal entities meet their predefined target regulatory solvency ratio over the medium term, 115 per cent[2] in Figure 6.2. The lower bound of the red zone is likely to be aligned with the minimum regulatory capital requirement for the entity, the level below which the entity wold be considered to be in breach of its regulatory requirements[3].

The 'amber trigger' is set at a level to be a prompt at which actions need to be considerd; the 'red thresholds' are positions that should not be breached and at which point action needs to be taken rather than just considered.

In calculating an entity's solvency position, mathematical models may allow for actions the company will take if certain agreed triggers are reached. These actions may include reducing bonuses for participating contracts and reducing the amount of risk-seeking assets within which the business is invested. As these actions give rise to the currently reported solvency position, it means that, as part of remaining at any given solvency ratio, these 'modelled' actions must be taken. If these actions are not taken, the solvency ratio should be reassessed as it would be materially worse than the level being reported. Conversely, taking these modelled actions earlier than planned can provide additional benefit. When the actual solvency ratio moves to a level outside the green zone, any action that is taken should aim to be sufficient to restore the solvency level to the target solvency ratio, not just back inside the green zone.

In setting the level of the buffer and the positions of the red, amber and green zones, consideration needs to be given to the number of additional 'unmodelled'[4] actions that are available and the speed with which the organisation is able to respond to circumstances as they evolve. This speed of response is as much about the quality, accuracy and frequency of the monitoring of the solvency position as how quickly actions can be implemented. If monitoring of solvency or time to implement actions were slow, an earlier higher boundary will be required to provide time for the business to resolve the position before the regulatory position is breached.

Within the Group outlined in Figure 6.1, it would be likely that each legal entity would be required to hold an amount of regulatory capital locally that assumes no benefit from being part of a Group. In addition to the regulatory capital requirement, the Group would agree with each entity a local target solvency ratio that included a small additional operational buffer[5] over and above the minimum regulatory requirement to ensure that the regulatory capital requirement is not breached by day-to-day fluctuations in the capital position (the operational buffer results in the 115 per cent target solvency ratio in Figure 6.2, rather than 100 per cent). Additionally, this operational buffer is held to reduce the frequency, and thus time and resources, with which legal entities engage the Group to request or return additional capital. In order to validate this efficiency saving and set the size of the buffer, the Group will consider a number of issues such as the planned capital requirements of the local entity given its growth plans, the quality and frequency of the local measurement of solvency (the better the tools, the more confidence in the reported position and the smaller the capital buffer can be), and how quickly capital can be moved around the Group.

Many Groups establish policies for managing the movement of capital and risk around the Group to ensure entities know how quickly financial resources can be provided and from where the Group will source the funds under various circumstances.

Following this assessment and allocation of capital, any excess capital is held at the Group centre to maximise the flexibility of an organisation to respond to events as they arise. A capital buffer at the Group will exist when the Group's total available capital is greater than the sum of the legal entity regulatory capital requirements plus the operational buffers. Figure 6.3 provides a worked illustration.

In Figure 6.3, the sum of the regulatory capital requirements (RCR) from the entities is greater than the RCR for the Group (that is, 100+200+500 is greater than 700). This is because there is the potential to diversify the capital requirement at the Group centre. However, for solvency purposes, this cannot generally be passed back to the units to enable them to hold a lower level of regulatory capital on an ongoing basis. The regulator is interested in ensuring that each entity on its own can meet its capital requirements should it be released by the Group. Hence, there is an amount of capital at the Group centre that becomes free as a result of diversification. In Figure 6.3, this is the 100 in the 'Group Total' column.

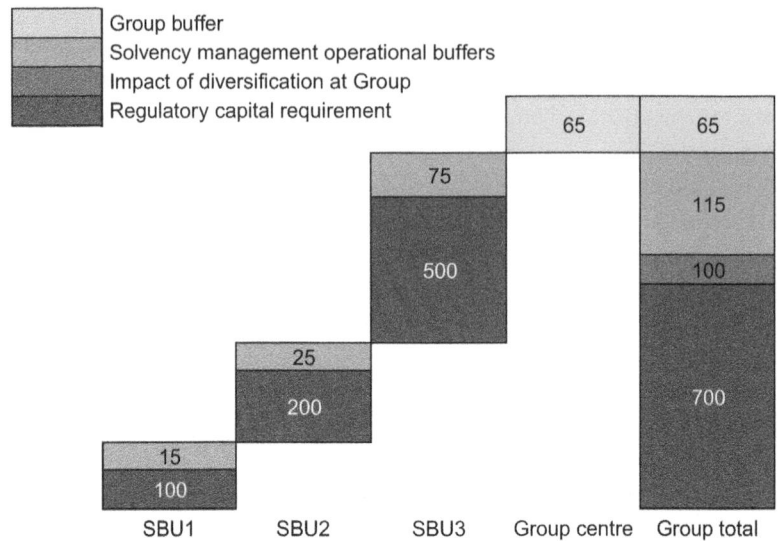

Figure 6.3   Worked example of local solvency and operational capital buffers

The management of the solvency position should include active management of both elements of the solvency ratio, the supply side (the quantity of capital available) and demand side (the amount of risk being taken). An alternative approach to moving capital around the business, is to move the risk to where the capital resides. This would mean effectively employing techniques such as swaps, reinsurance or outsourcing arrangements from the local entity to the Group centre. The approach reduces the demand for capital movements to support solvency as the volatility of local entity balance sheets is reduced.

A number of multinationals have been seeking to improve financial efficiency and flexibility by reducing the number of legal entities within their corporate structure. Many seek the 'holy grail' of a single balance sheet. Some of the major considerations in consolidating legal entities have been

- dealing with the tax implications of moving between local regulatory and tax regimes;
- deploying capital to the most capital efficient locations, avoiding dividend traps[6] and ensuring capital can be redeployed as quickly as possible to where the Group needs it;
- ensuring that capital can return to the Group, sufficiently to pay investor coupons, dividends and maturities, and to facilitate share buy-back arrangements.

These projects to improve capital efficiency also investigate potential risk transfer structures, such as implementing reinsurance captives at the Group Centre, to ensure risk transfer mechanisms can be deployed if moving capital between entities is not the most efficient approach.

6.2 Operationalising economic capital management

In Figure 6.3, the Group has allocated physical resources to each legal entity equivalent to the regulatory requirements of each entity plus an operational buffer of capital. This operational buffer of capital is not the same as the amount of economic capital required by the business. As the Group Centre reports the Group's overall solvency position, it too has a solvency ratio that it needs to manage. However, as this is the overarching solvency position, its target solvency position *will* be the same as the economic capital target determined from the risk appetite statements. As the Group's solvency management corridor is determined from the overarching risk limits that have been established, the Group's solvency management corridor is also the Group's economic capital management corridor.

Where there is reasonable alignment between the regulatory regime and the economic basis underpinning the internal economic capital view, expressing the economic capital requirement as a buffer over and above the regulatory capital requirement (a multiple of Group diversified regulatory capital requirement) makes the monitoring of solvency and economic capital positions easier and reduces the complexity of having to calculate and manage too many different metrics. This approach also ensures that if the Group manages its economic capital within the capital management corridor, then the Group will be meeting its regulatory solvency requirement.

Figure 6.4 illustrates a capital management corridor approach. The Group's capital management corridor will appear similar to the local entities' solvency management corridors, but the triggers and thresholds will be set at different levels. In this example, the economic capital requirement is expressed as 140 per cent of the regulatory capital requirement.

Figure 6.4 illustrates amber and red corridors above the target solvency level as well as below it. The corridors above the target solvency level exist because not fully utilising capital is inefficient and can lead to a drag on return. In the longer term, having too much capital can lead to a demand for a return of excess capital to those who provided it, or a reduction in the propensity of the organisation to attract shareholders, who may view the organisation as too risk averse and the associated return too low.

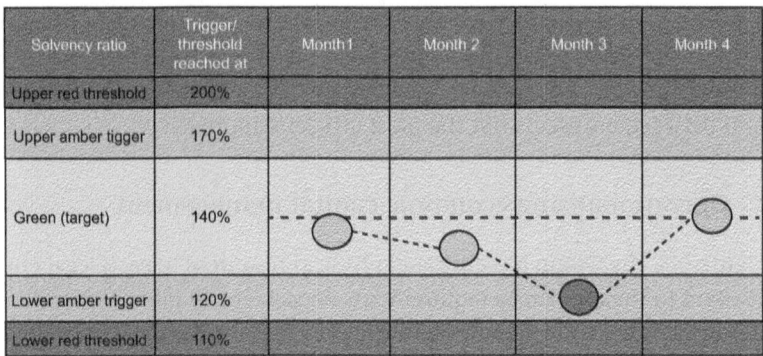

Solvency ratio	Trigger/ threshold reached at	Month 1	Month 2	Month 3	Month 4
Upper red threshold	200%				
Upper amber tigger	170%				
Green (target)	140%				
Lower amber trigger	120%				
Lower red threshold	110%				

Figure 6.4 The Group's capital management corridor

The aim of capital management is to hold sufficient capital to support the economic capital requirements on average over the medium term. Any actions to restore the target economic capital level should factor in a medium-term time horizon in the basis for assessing their impact. This means that both on a daily basis and for periods over the planning horizon, the Group may have more or less than this medium-term target amount.

While the amount of actual economic capital being held may fluctuate over time, performance, initiatives and products should always be assessed assuming they are charged for the target level of economic capital, irrespective of the actual level of capital that the Group or a business unit holds.

6.3   Allocating economic capital to business units

Allocations of financial resources for the purposes of managing solvency are physical movements of resources. Allocations of economic capital from the Group are notional allocations for the purposes of risk management.

As the allocation of economic capital is notional, it is possible to allocate this capital through a framework that fits with the approach used internally for the management of the Group, which can be different from that required by the structure of the legal entities. For example, the structure in Figure 6.1 illustrates three legal entities potentially differing by geographical location. The Group may manage its risks through a management view with two businesses, life and general insurance, and thus choose to allocate its economic capital via this latter structure[7].

The next phase of capital management planning is to allocate economic capital to these business units and establish the risk limit framework (green zone, amber triggers and red thresholds). Allocating economic capital to the various business units and establishing risk limits incorporates a number of key considerations:

1. the return on capital, potential volatility of that return and the length of time over which the allocation of capital will, by necessity of the term of contracts that are written, be put out to work;
2. the capabilities of the executive team to manage the risks effectively;
3. the actions the business can and is willing to take in order to manage its allocation of economic capital within any boundaries given;
4. how the diversification benefit from being part of a Group is allocated down to the business units and risk types, such that it rewards those that give rise to the benefit of diversification.

   Diversification is an important benefit of being part of a Group and needs to be shared with the business units to ensure they gain competitively from this attribute through being able to price products with a lower capital requirement. Sharing the diversification benefit with business units provides an incentive for business units to think about the Group as a whole and target a risk profile that supports diversification at a Group level, reducing capital costs for the Group as a whole, which, when allocated back down to the businesses, makes their products carry a lower charge for capital usage. For this reason, it is important to ensure that a method of allocation is applied that identifies the sources of the diversification benefit and can allocate the benefit back to the exposures, appropriately resulting in lowering the capital requirement associated with the risks that give rise to the diversification.
5. As the economic capital calculation is applied over a business planning cycle in which it is expected that new business will be written and some in-force business may mature and 'go off the books', any calculation needs to make allowance for both movements (planned levels of new business and in-force business exits) and then be fixed for the year[8]. It should be noted that while the overall budget for the year is fixed, the evolution of that budget over the year should move dynamically, as the business is expected to come on and go off the books. Allocating the full fixed budget at outset would mean that excessive risk-taking might occur at the start of the year.

6.4   Establishing the economic capital management corridors (risk limits and tolerances)

Having finalised the overarching solvency and capital management corridors, it is necessary to cascade these down into more granular operational limits. These operational limits provide boundaries on the risk-taking and allow business units to operate relatively independently on a day-to-day basis, while ensuring the Group, overall, operates within the constraints specified by the risk appetite statements.

In setting the operational limits it should be borne in mind that the risk appetite statements are the strategic medium-term aims, with the risk tolerances or operational limits more short-term tactical boundaries.

The operational limits need to be set at levels that encourage active risk-return optimisation, narrow enough to ensure active management of the exposure, and wide enough to allow for day-to-day market fluctuations to occur without management having to take actions with an unreasonable frequency.

When deciding the width of the ranges, certain questions must be considered

1. How often do you undertake full calculations or receive information such that you have an accurate understanding of the risk position?
2. How accurate is your 'proxy modelling'?
3. How does the frequency with which you monitor and report exposures change as you get nearer any limits?
4. How quickly can the adverse events materialise?
5. Can you respond to restore the capital position or continue with your business plans if resources fall to the levels established by the ranges?
6. How quickly can you respond with actions to a deteriorating position, for example such as solvency getting close to the minimum regulatory requirement?
7. How long will it take for actions to have an impact and restore the earnings level, for example?
8. Who is responsible for mitigating risks, and when are issues escalated to senior management?

Once the risk limits have been established, it is important to undertake some stress and scenario testing to ensure that when the organisation reaches the red thresholds, the diversification benefit that is assumed to exist has not changed too much. If this is the case, the limits may need to be re-assessed, as the nature of the interactions and capital requirements would appear to be changing too dynamically in these scenarios for the limits to remain as a reliable indicator of the risk exposure and underlying solvency position.

7
Risk and Capital Modelling

This chapter provides coverage of the components of risk and capital models to understand how experts can be challenged in order to gain insights to the limitations of the modelling output and enhance the application of judgment in decision making. In particular, the chapter will

– discuss the purpose of a model and its shortcomings,
– explain various balance sheets and their purpose,
– explain the components of the model and how to challenge the data and parameterisation.

7.1 Background

All models are wrong, but some are useful – George Box

Why do models exist and what issues surround their use?

Businesses operate in the real world. However, in order to try to work out how much to charge for products and services, and how much to set aside to meet future obligations, we try to build models that replicate what happens in the real world, to convert complex interactions into a financial value.

Building these models requires us to convert reality into things mathematical so that they can be simulated and linked together to reflect interactions. We make assumptions about behaviours and environments, simplifying the complex interactions and emotions that drive the real world. As events occur in day-to-day life, the real world does not know or understand these mathematical representations, as they do not actually exist. Probabilities do not exist or act on objects in the real world. We need to remember that the model does not drive real world behaviours.

Mathematics is someone's simplified subjective representation of observations of a world that is irrational, sentimental and behaves illogically. Confusion arises when mathematics is assumed to be part of what drives real-world events and behaviours.

To illustrate the importance of the assumptions and simplifications we make, take the example of a simple toss of a coin. Most people would say there is a 50 per cent chance of its landing as a head and 50 per cent chance of its landing as a tail. Most notably, we have immediately made some assumptions about the environment for this experiment and used our prior experiences to come to this conclusion. Implicitly, we have done several things:

1. We have made assumptions about the coin. The coin could land on its edge, and the dimensions of the coin could make this more or less likely.
2. We have assumed that the action of tossing the coin does not interfere with the eventual outcome.
3. We have assumed the environment in which the coin is tossed allows it to fall without interference.
4. We have assumed the surface on which the coin will land is flat and does not introduce another outcome or make it more material (such as an uneven surface or rocks that make it more likely it could land on its side).
5. We have limited our scope of thought on potential outcomes because in our past experiences and those of our friends, we have never experienced a coin landing on its edge, and so our historical data set, while extensive, does not contain evidence of this outcome and thus it will not appear in extrapolations of the historical data.

While this example is overplayed here, it highlights the importance of understanding the relevance of the implicit assumptions made and the need to apply non-mathematical reasoning to understand events that may not exist in the data that is available, and the basis of our own prior experiences. This is the key to a good risk and capital model, that is, the understanding of what has been assumed, what the model does not capture, and under what circumstances these issues and simplifications may become materially misleading.

To add to the complexity between reality and the modelled worlds, money, technically, has no intrinsic value. It acquires a value through the association with the procurement of basic needs such as food, and as a method for exchange in which we can acquire something on which we place a value and defer settlement, through the provision of goods or services, to a time when the provider has a need. Using a medium of exchange is a personal expression of the minimum immediate utility of a good or service. The utility and hence the 'value' which individuals place on goods and services will differ over time, and will change as individuals' own circumstances, attitude towards events and personal preferences change. This is why people react differently to different events. The difficulty is that in order to model the 'market place' for what we offer, we need to group these people together into an homogeneous mass and make assumptions about their attitude towards utility, 'value' and thus, how they behave, in order to produce something to guide our actions in the real world.

Models are becoming more and more complex as experts seek ways to improve their ability to 'predict' this reality. The complex real-world environment in which we interact is not underpinned by a set of rules, but is driven by sentimental human decision-making. Many authors criticise the risk and capital models used during the financial crisis as not accounting for the possibility of 'fat tails'. Their issue is about whether financial market movements can be represented by certain mathematical distributions, or representations of ranges of potential outcomes, with the aim of estimating the extreme potential losses. To some extent, this view misses the point and the value of a model.

A model can inform us about what would have happened in previous scenarios and the relative importance of the various risks that a company faces. By using consistent sources of information for parameterisation time and again, a model can tell us whether the extent of a risk exposure has moved materially from its previous position. Thus, model output is just a relative measure of how an exposure changes through time that can provide a basis around which to structure discussions. Problems arise when models are actively 'squeezed' to justify the volume of risk-taking or become the sole justification for following a course of action.

This was the problem with subprime lending in the United States ahead of the credit crisis of 2008, when investment banks chased return on the basis that the models said it was a low-risk business. Effectively, chief executive officers (CEOs) found something that justified writing a block of business in huge quantities, and the natural herd mentality meant most companies followed suit.

This highlights an area of concern for a risk manager – if a huge notional position is built up based on a small probability of an adverse outcome, its net exposure may look small, but what if that small probability is wrong? This is one of the lessons to be learned from the crisis of 2008, and the reason why attempting to reduce risk management to a single statistic is extremely dangerous. The desire for a utopia of a single value, such as 'value-at-risk' on which to base risk decisions, is in danger of becoming a holy grail that blinds Boards from establishing proper diverse risk management techniques and the application of experienced judgment.

Potentially, part of the desire for a single statistic has arisen because technological evolution has increased the speed and breadth of information exchanges, and facilitated easier settlement of exchanges of goods and services. In turn, this has shortened the time frames within which managers are pressured to make decisions and interpret the irrational, sentimental and illogical. Thus, it is easiest for managers to rationalise decisions by following the herd and the model. This is compounded by the public and media that can benchmark managers against each other and create sentiment that can have significant implications for managers' careers and long-term earnings. This reinforces managers' desire to act in self-interest and return a performance in line with the market, good or bad, as this is a safe option for them personally. This is why we get investment bubbles.

This supports the view that the failings are not of the models, but of human behaviour. People use models without understanding the shortcomings or 'game' the model to justify what they do. This would suggest it is the application of business sense and ethics that fails and why an understanding of the business and the model are equally important.

> Consider this: would you put someone, who did not know how to drive, in charge of a bus on a fast-flowing freeway?

In the early 2000s, investment products were designed for companies by developing a proposition that 'arbitraged' the models that were being used, such that the product produced a perceived enhanced return at a lower level of risk.

This ability to use data to justify a position is not new. Consider legal processes in which there is always a doctor or subject matter expert who is available to support a position on a case.

Conversely, people can ignore data to justify actions. Even an expert's ability to estimate risk is limited by what psychologists call 'probability neglect', that is, a tendency to ignore statistics when emotions are high. This has implications when assessing catastrophic risks for which the enormity of the outcome can blind the assessor to the small probability of its occurrence. This assessment can be further distorted by fear and irrational behaviour created by hyped publicity and media representations. For example, the aim of terrorists is to create an extreme picture of an event to generate fear in order to achieve a change in a pattern of behaviour or a specific outcome. The fear generated by the visualisation of the horrific outcome results in the likelihood of the occurrence of a terrorist act being less relevant in people's minds when deciding how to behave, thus achieving the terrorists desired end-state.

This ability both to find supporting evidence for assumptions and neglect evidence because of emotion highlight why the use of data and an understanding of the application of expert judgment are important areas for Boards to be able to challenge in order to understand the assumptions made in models and know how to manage risks. This challenge process is about ensuring that Boards understand explicitly the assumptions that experts make implicitly in coming to any position or recommendation and attempting to remove emotion from the calibration and decision making processes.

Experts who develop models need to explain the 'unknowns' or uncertainties in the models so that Boards can make well-reasoned decisions about risk that will never come solely from mathematical models.

In order for Boards to make decisions without being blinded by the complexity of mathematics, a reasoned application of judgment needs to be grounded in an understanding of the components of the model, the nature of simplifications and what has been assumed in order to produce the parameterisation for the model. The following section outlines what is being modelled and how the components of this model are derived.

7.2   What are we trying to model and how can we challenge it?

Firstly, why do models exist and what are we trying to extract from them?

At the basic level, the model is used to determine the amount of capital available on a balance sheet that is not needed to meet any obligations or other requirements. But there are multiple balance sheets produced for different purposes and stakeholders, including

1. regulatory returns – These are for the regulator and are used to assess whether the business has sufficient money available to withstand a reasonably adverse event and has time to invoke a run-off plan to secure the obligations from the contracts written to date to which the company is still exposed. For market-consistent approaches such as Europe's Solvency 2, the parameterisation of the model is about making sure that the company has enough capital to buy the insurance required to minimise the risks in order to meet the promises that the company has made to customers that

have contracts with it now. This insurance may be in the form of financial instruments, such as put options, or reinsurance. The buffer is also the level at which the regulator knows it must start to get much closer to the company and its plans in order to ensure that management is actively resolving its financial position and understands the point at which it is appropriate to accept the closing of the business.

2. projections of the economic balance sheet – This is a projection of the internal view of the true underlying economics of the business that is used for the purposes of business planning. The aim is to assess the implications of growing the business over the plan horizon at the proposed rate. This is the view that provides the Board with an understanding of the affordability of the plan and the risks that are being taken to deliver it. This view can differ from the regulatory view of the balance sheet, as it allows for the projected volumes of new business that is expected to be written and is not constrained by accounting or regulatory rules.

7.2.1   Explanation of the balance sheets

To understand the components of a balance sheet, we shall start by assessing the returns we provide to the regulator. Please remember that these explanations are simplifications that focus on the high-level concepts and not the technical details. As such, approaches may differ by territory.

Simply stated, a balance sheet is

Assets – liabilities – a buffer = solvency position

Different regulatory regimes specify their own approach to calculating each of the components, some of which are more prescriptive than others. A number of these are outlined in the following sections.

7.2.1.1   *Solvency 1*

'Solvency 1' is the pan-European regulatory basis, which is planned for replacement by the new 'Solvency 2' regime. Solvency 1 is heavily formulaic, and has been criticised extensively for not being risk sensitive.

Generally, assets are valued at market value, and there are deductions, limits and restrictions on the amounts that certain assets can count as available in the assessment.

The liabilities are based on the policies that are in force at the date of the assessment. We must assess the potential future claims that are likely to arise from the business, and can offset this by the premium income we expect to receive from these policies. In addition, we must hold sufficient capital to meet the expenses that are expected to arise in the future as we manage this business, but we cannot take credit for any future expense-saving strategies.

In setting the assumptions underlying these calculations, we must determine a best estimate of what we think might happen and add a margin for prudence.

As the calculations work out how much we must hold now for events that might occur in the future, we are allowed to make allowance for interest that we can earn on the money we put aside today. There are very specific rules about how to calculate this interest rate, taking account of the assets we hold, which is a key driver of the value of the liabilities.

When we write a policy, we expect to incur upfront costs, but to recoup these over the lifetime of the policy from the profits we expect to make. We cannot take credit fully for the future profits we expect to make on business we have written, and can only take account of the cash flows as they arise. Hence, if a company writes a lot of business, it can lead to a deterioration of the solvency position.

7.2.1.2 Solvency 2

Simply put, a Solvency 2 balance sheet is the same, that is,

Assets – liabilities – a buffer = solvency position

Assets are valued at market value and some deductions, limits and restrictions exist that can impact the assets that can count as available for certain purposes[1]. These adjustments are different from those applied under Solvency 1. In addition, the stream of future profits that are expected to arise on business that has been written can be recognised on the balance sheet.

In assessing the stream of future profits and the amount of liabilities, cash flow forecasts are produced. Where appropriate, the cash flows allow for the contractual benefits to change over time as economic conditions change. Cash flows are projected for the lifetime of each policy. In cases in which companies have written large volumes of business, these calculations can take a long time to undertake; therefore, sometimes a number of sample policies are created that represent the business in aggregate. These are referred to as model points. It is important that these model points collectively reflect the nature of the business that has been written.

In setting the assumptions underlying these cash flow calculations, we must determine our estimate of what we think will happen, where possible, in a manner consistent with the approaches used in the financial markets. For example, if we have written a contract that behaves like a put option, we should value the contract in the same way in which the financial market would value a put option[2]. Further, we do not need to add a margin for prudence.

In performing these calculations, we are able to make allowance for what we would expect to do in the future, these being agreed 'management actions'.

In this assessment, the interest rate assumption is sometimes referred to as the 'risk-free' rate, or the 'reference' rate. The rate is reflective of the approach to discounting used in financial markets for instruments that are relevant to the nature of the liabilities that have been written.

The buffer is determined by aggregating the results from a number of 'what if...?' scenarios. These 'what if...?' scenarios can be either those that have been prescribed by regulation (standard formula), or those determined from internal analysis if the regulator believes these to be justified and appropriate (internal model). In aggregate, these 'what if...?' scenarios should determine the amount of capital that a company requires to be at least as financially strong as a company with a credit rating of 'BBB'.

7.2.1.3   US (NAIC) regulations

The National Association of Insurance Commissioners (NAIC) regulations are being reviewed and evolved. However, in simple terms, the balance sheet is the same:

Assets – liabilities – a buffer = solvency position

Generally, assets are valued at market value, and there are deductions, limits and restrictions on the amounts that certain assets can count as available in the assessment.

For non-variable annuity business, the liabilities are valued using a prescribed approach that does not allow explicitly for all cash flows such as expenses, but makes implicit prudent adjustments. Certain of the assumptions are prescribed by the regulator, including mortality tables and maximum interest rates[3] that can be used.

Variable annuity business is valued in a manner consistent with approaches used in financial markets, with certain elements prescribed by the regulator.

The buffer capital is calculated by aggregating a number of 'what if...?' scenarios that are prescribed by the regulator.

7.2.1.4   Projected internal economic balance sheet

The regulatory balance sheets are potentially different from the internal economic balance sheet used for business planning purposes. If we assume that the regulatory balance sheet has an underlying economic basis, the nature of areas of difference may be:

- The regulatory balance sheet may not be concerned with future levels of new business, and hence, there may be different assumptions about the costs of managing the business into the future and the potential for new business to generate economies of scale;
- Reporting standards may not require certain expenses to be accounted for within the base balance sheet, such as future project costs or discretionary staff bonuses. However, when projecting the balance sheet for planning purposes, these may need to be allowed for;
- Regulatory balance sheets assess the capital required to buy insurance and hedge out the balance sheet. The cost of insurance is likely to be at a premium to actual underlying expected experience (that is, include a margin for expenses, the cost of capital and profit). This means that to the extent that insurance has not been purchased, these margins would unwind to the company over time.
- Regulatory balance sheets may have prescriptive rules about the method of calculation or the parameterisation of certain aspects, such as the rate for the cost of capital and approaches to allow for the obligations to, and the loss-absorbing nature of funds provided by the capital markets. These should be replaced with the internal view, and any margin (or loss) should fall to the cash flow in the period. Additionally, the regulatory balance sheet may require that a company err on the side of prudence, and thus, a company may deem it appropriate to release these prudent margins in their assumptions about economic best estimate.
- Some regulatory approaches use the term 'market consistent' to relate to the balance sheet.

But for market consistency, with which market is it appropriate to be consistent?

Generally, the term 'market consistent' has been used to relate to marking the approach to valuing liabilities to that used in a liquid financial market that settles payments immediately in cash. However, a view may be taken that this market is not consistent with the nature of the liabilities that a company writes – the nature of the liabilities is such that they would be extremely unlikely to be settled for cash immediately. Hence, we need to adjust the calculations to value the liabilities using an approach, discount rate in particular, that more closely reflects this nature. This is the underpinning of the debate about the 'illiquidity premium' on annuity business in particular. Again, the internal view may differ in this area from the regulatory requirements.

– The regulatory balance sheet requires the company to hold a buffer of capital against adverse events. For various reasons outlined in the capital risk appetite statement discussion in Section 4.3, the internal view may be to hold a larger capital buffer.

In the European Solvency 2 regime, these internal economic projections underpin the Own Risk and Solvency Assessment.

7.2.2   Components of a model

The following section outlines how a model is developed to quantify the elements of the equation;

Assets – liabilities – a buffer = solvency position

A model builds representations of the assets and liabilities that the company holds or expects to have in the future.

Assets: The approach to modelling the assets may vary, but effectively, the model should be able to

– value an asset in a manner consistent with how it would be valued in the financial markets,
– allow for the nature and timing of any cash flows from the assets, with
– the associated costs of investment, and any taxes due, for example, on income.

For projections into the future, the model will need to make assumptions about how cash inflows will be reinvested and assets will be valued in various future time periods. There may be assumptions about

– how assets arising from future new business that is written are invested, which need to be understood relative to the assumptions made in pricing new business, and
– changes in the mix of assets backing in-force savings business that need to be consistent with the basis provided to customers through information and illustrations.

It may not be feasible to model each asset individually, and thus, similar to the approach taken to value liabilities, the assets may have been 'bucketed together' into a smaller number of representative assets, or asset model points. This may be, for example, into groups of bonds by credit rating and term, and equities by representative indexes, such as the FTSE 100, Dow Jones and DAX.

Liabilities: For the liabilities, a model attempts to represent the cash flows that an organisation expects to occur over the coming years from the business it has written, these cash flows being premiums received, expenses incurred, claims paid, tax, and so on.

If a significant number of policies has been written, it may not be feasible to assess each one individually, instead the policies being represented by a smaller number of representative 'model points'.

The next layer of complexity is added by acknowledging that the world does not behave in a 'deterministic' way (that is, an assumption that there is a single possible outcome of the future), but that there is a range of possible outcomes in future years. This is stochastic modelling. The economic scenario generator (ESG) is a tool that uses mathematical techniques to produce this range of possible future investment market performance outcomes that are then used in the model. These modelling techniques can be extended to areas other than financial markets in which the future outcome may lie within a range of possible outcomes (for example, mortality). It is important that the ESG is parameterised in a way that its output is representative of the nature and term of the liabilities, and is able to produce reasonable valuations of the company's assets.

The final layer is a result of the range of future outcomes that we highlighted previously, in that we would behave differently in each of these future economic scenarios. For example, if the solvency of the company were threatened, management would take action to batten down the hatches and reduce the company's risk-taking, and customers might change their behaviour. This is an example of modelling 'management's actions and customer behaviour'.

Questions for the Board: In developing models that are proportionate to a business, it is sometimes necessary to simplify the products and the assets that are modelled and not represent features that are viewed as not material.

- For a Board member, is it clear which aspects of products and assets are not represented in the models and how this has been justified?
- As models have adopted stochastic elements, companies have relied more and more on outsourced providers for calibrations of tools such as ESGs. Is it clear what data has been used for these calibrations and how these have been checked for appropriateness to the organisation?
- As many companies cannot process each single asset and policy through their calculation system, the assets and policies are grouped into

'representative' forms. How have Board members become comfortable with the groupings applied to the assets and liabilities as being representative of the full business? How have Board members become comfortable with the groupings being appropriate representations of the business under extreme stressed conditions? (For some product types, their nature or exposure may change under severe economic conditions and therefore distort the results from a particular grouping.)

–   Finally, how have Board members become comfortable with the idea that the application of the behaviour of customers and management's actions within the model are cutting in where the company expects and having the appropriate affect?

7.2.3   The assets and liabilities – parameterising the model

Having considered the components used to construct the model, we need to parameterise the model.

The cash flows in a model are usually determined based on a combination of information we know and information we do not know with certainty. For example,

–   we may have agreed to pay £50,000 if someone dies, but do not know when he or she will die;
–   we know what it cost to administer the business last year, but do not know exactly what it will cost in the coming years.

It is the aspects of the cash flows we do not know with certainty that give rise to the risks we face. These are parameterised by making assumptions. What we do, or assume, in order to come up with our best estimates for these parameters are the things we can get wrong, that could change over time in a way we did not expect, or change in value in a more volatile way year-on-year than we expected.

In order to estimate the uncertainty that exists in these dimensions, we need to understand what drives the potential areas of uncertainty. These are sometimes referred to as the 'risk drivers' and may come from

1. the relevance of the data to the underlying item being parameterised – For example, as a result of a lack of data for subprime lending, collateralised debt obligations (CDOs) on subprime mortgages were priced assuming the default rates, loss given default and prepayment risks were similar to those of prime mortgages, for which there was more data. However, as it turned out, those individuals who bought subprime mortgages behaved differently from prime borrowers, and

the environment in which subprime lending occurred (for example, reduced checking of affordability) meant the assumptions were not fit for purpose.

2. the volume of data available – For example, because the likelihood of someone dying is relatively small, it is necessary to build up a large pool of data to enable the experience that comes from that business to be sufficient so that any conclusions can be drawn from that data with a reasonable degree of certainty. If you have ten policies and no one died in a year, it does not mean that no one will ever die in any future year, so
   – How do you set your best estimate of the future?
   – At what point does a volume of data become reliable enough for it to be used as a basis for setting parameters?
   There are a number of standard statistical tests that have been developed to infer a level of confidence that the data gives a reasonable indication from which a model can be parameterised.

3. the number of years of historic data available – This is connected with establishing a sufficient volume of data from which to draw conclusions with confidence. The differences between the business and the environment going forward, and that which existed at the time relevant to the data being sourced need to be considered and appropriate adjustments made, with the rationale and implications of such decisions explained.

4. what may be missing from the data – As in the example of the coin toss, judgment needs to be applied to consider what could happen that is not represented in the data available to date.

5. the potential for external events to impact the underlying drivers of the experience from the data available – For example, it may be that we expect an improvement in the ability to treat cancer going forward, such that we expect people will have a prolongation of life and we will see fewer deaths at earlier ages from a particular cause of cancer than has been the case in the past.

6. extending the data to provide insight to potential extremely adverse changes in these parameters, requires finding a way of creating an extension of the data set in a way that looks reasonable – For example, we have seen few 1-in-200-year events and thus to establish what such an event could be requires some sensible way of extending the data we have into 'synthetically' created extreme possibilities.

7.2.3.1   *The liabilities – understanding the best estimate of the liabilities*

We need to hold sufficient assets to meet the promises we have made to our customers and suppliers, and have enough to pay the salaries and other benefits of the staff that we need to manage the business over the period in which we expect to be making these payments. This is because we write contracts that might, for example, become payable in ten years' time, and we need to ensure someone is employed to meet this obligation at that time. The term 'best estimate' is sometimes used interchangeably with the term 'market consistent'. However, it should be noted that these two terms might not relate to the same result. Best estimate can be used to refer to the assessment of historic experience from the data that is available, whereas market consistent refers to the price that the financial market would charge to insure the risk to the balance sheet.

There are various terms used to describe the amount of money required to meet these obligations including 'liabilities', 'reserves' and 'provisions'. To determine the appropriate parameters on which to base the calculations for the amount of provisions to be held, it is necessary to assess three key elements:

 (i) experience relating to the business that has been written,
 (ii) the experience of financial markets,
(iii) the required expenses for managing the business over the future years.

(i) *Experience relating to the business that has been written.*   The parameters related to the expected experience[4] from the business that has been written can be determined using various sources of data:

– general market data, such as population statistics or standard actuarial tables;
– reinsurers' data based on experience from their own portfolio or their own research;
– experience of products or portfolios with similar exposures;
– analysis of the experience of the company's own portfolio.

When using any form of data, the Board needs to consider the appropriateness of the data for the purpose for which it is being used and the confidence that the Board can place in the experience being replicated within their business going forward.

For example, some of the considerations would include whether

1. the data is relevant to the underlying business to which the parameterisation is being applied;
2. circumstances that were driving the previous experience have changed, or will change;

3. the analysis of experience shows results in a way that may be distorting the picture of the true underlying risks; for example, whether claims experience is presented by the number of claims and whether any distortions exist because of the size of policies;
4. reinsurance rates have been used to establish the basis for best estimate assumptions. The reinsurer is likely to have won a tender process by being cheaper than competitors. Do you understand the difference in views of future experience between the selected reinsurer and others?

(ii) *The experience of financial markets.* A number of the assumptions in the model, such as future investment returns and inflation, require information from the financial markets. For those using stochastic modelling techniques, the main of these assumptions will underpin the range of financial outcomes projected from the ESG. The ESG is a tool that is used to project forward a range of economic variables (for example, asset returns, interest rates) over a long-term horizon. For each of the economic variables, a mathematical model is chosen that is perceived to provide the best representation of the range of scenarios that could arise into the future given the historic behaviour of that variable. The ESG tool generates a number of scenarios that allow us to value the options and guarantees we have provided on policies in a manner consistent with how financial markets value assets that exhibit similar features. To a large extent, the questions of the Board are similar to those for challenging the data used to set the parameters for the underlying business experience.

For example,

1. what is the relevance of the underlying data that has been modelled to the portfolio of assets actually held by the business? For example, if the company holds equity from a mix of countries and these are modelled using a single equity index, is the index representative of the performance of the underlying equity holdings from the various countries?
2. how have each of the models that projects forward the economic variables been chosen and made relevant to both the company's business and the financial market?
3. how do these individual models for interest rates and equity, for example, interact or interrelate?
4. how does the pricing of financial instruments from the model compare with the market values of instruments that we have already?
5. how has any illiquidity premium been derived? How has any historic data been adjusted for future economic and financial conditions?

6. if the basis of the projections is such that the output is meant to be market consistent, does the investment team believe it can go out and buy the appropriate instruments for the price being calculated?

(iii) *Expense projections.* Projecting expenses can be one of the most challenging areas for the models, as it is usually one of the most underdeveloped. Setting these parameters can be one of the most contentious areas of basis setting. This is because expenses that are associated with the ongoing maintenance of the business have to be provisioned for each year in which they are expected to arise. However, one-off projects or expenses associated with acquiring new business do not need to be provisioned for each year into the future (as these are deemed to be able to be ceased when new business is curtailed).

As a simplified example,

– if the cost of maintaining a contract was £1 a year and the contract was for ten years, it would be necessary to set aside £10 for maintenance costs, whereas
– if the costs associated with acquiring a contract were £1, as the regulatory view does not assume future new business is written, it would only be necessary to set aside say £1 for the costs associated with acquisitions.

Hence, it is possible to obtain an optically stronger balance sheet by having more expenses allocated to acquisition and one-off projects than to business maintenance activity.

Furthermore, the expenses associated with maintaining the business are likely to increase each year in line with inflation (at a rate based on a mix of general inflation and salary inflation, depending on the proportion of the cost base resulting from employee-related costs).

The company's cost base will be made up of costs that are assumed to be fixed and that do not vary with the volume of business in force (for example, costs associated with providing regulatory returns each year), and costs that do vary as business volumes change (for example, customer service costs). If these costs are converted into a cost per policy, consideration needs to be given to the projected policy count over the coming years. This is because a declining volume of policies in-force will result in each policy having to cover a greater proportion of the fixed cost each year into the future (that is, a reflection of reducing economies of scale). This will increase the implied inflation rate per policy, and it needs to be factored into the overall assessment of the inflation rate. Conversely, projections that include new business to the extent that the volume of policies in force is increasing over time, will see the opposite effect. In these scenarios, care needs to be taken when this adjustment for increasing economies of scale is based on aggressive assumptions about the level of new business growth.

7.2.4 The assets and liabilities – allowing for the impact of management actions and policyholder behaviour

The model can make allowance for actions that management would take under various scenarios, such as how assets will be reinvested when redemptions arise and changing the investment mix as the solvency position declines.

Similarly, the models will make allowances for policyholder behaviour. For example, in scenarios in which stock markets fall, customers may have an increased propensity to let their policy lapse.

In order to ensure that management is comfortable with the allowance for changes in policyholder behaviour and the benefits being taken for management actions, consideration should be given to questions such as:

Management actions

1. Is the management action fair to policyholders and in line with any expectation that the company may have created?
2. Is this an action that you would take? Is the Board signed up to do this?
3. Under what conditions would you do this and what are the trigger points? Has the potential action been in place for a while, and have triggers been exceeded but no action taken previously?
4. Are there scenarios in which the action would not be able to be taken or not realise the value that is being put forward? How has this been factored into the assessment?
5. Does a plan exist as to how the action will be executed and what sort of time frame is involved? How have any delays in execution been factored into the assessment?

Policyholder behaviour

1. On what basis have you drawn the link between the circumstances and why policyholders will behave as you infer?
2. What assumptions are you making in drawing this conclusion and how are you monitoring the continued appropriateness?

When considering making allowance for management actions, it is necessary to consider the wider implications and any additional adjustments that need to be made. The following example illustrates the risks entailed in not considering the wider implications of management actions.

– A company competed in the annuity market. At the time, one of the major components of the investment strategy was to invest in corporate bonds. This means that two of the key assumptions, particularly in pricing, are the assessment of the risk from defaults on the corporate bonds and the size of any loss associated with a default.

In order to reduce the number of defaults allowed within the assumptions, the commercial team priced assuming that all bonds were sold when they were downgraded to below 'BBB', thus mitigating a default. This meant that they priced in a lower chance of default occurring. However, the pricing failed to recognise that in selling the bonds and reinvesting the proceeds, they were effectively crystallising a loss at the point at which the bond was sold. Although the loss may not be as large as that likely to occur if they held it to default, it was missing from the pricing parameters, and thus, the assessment of the profitability of the business was somewhat erroneous.

As part of assessing the wider implications of management actions, it is important to consider whether the management actions being implemented create any new risks. This is particularly important when considering actions to mitigate risks arising from human behaviours, as human behaviours have a tendency to change in a bid to beat any system that is put in place to prevent or monitor the threat they create.

For example, introducing counterterrorism techniques at airports check-ins might not mitigate the terrorism risk completely, but could result in terrorists reacting by changing tactics and switching targets to aim for naval ports or railway stations.

This behavioural trait is not one you would experience from a naturally occurring event such as a flood, in which you have little ability to prevent the incident from happening or to control its magnitude. However, you may be able to provide early warning signals and create barriers to mitigate the impact in key areas, but the flood will not take actions to avoid the mitigants you have put in place.

7.2.5   The buffer – calculating the buffer capital requirement using value at risk (VaR)

Having built and parameterised the model, we need to determine the tests that will be used and applied to the parameters in the model to calculate the buffer capital requirement, in this example, through the assessment of the value at risk (VaR).

Simply put, the VaR figure is a change in the value of the capital available on a balance sheet that results from a change in a parameter value specified in a 'what if...?' scenario. These 'what if...?' scenarios are based on extremely adverse but plausible events. As there are many types of risk exposures and risk drivers, a number of 'what if...?' scenarios are developed, the results from which are aggregated in a way that allows for the degree to which these events may interact (that is, one event occurs, leading to another event happening). The aggregated result of the 'what if...?' scenarios forms the buffer capital requirement. The 'what if...?' scenarios are key to the internal economic capital assessment and in the internal model under a Solvency 2 framework.

The 'what if...?' scenarios form the stress tests used to calculate the capital requirements for risk categories such as market, credit and demographic risks. For example, the stress test could be 'what if the equity markets fell by 40 per cent?' The parameterisation of the 'what if...?' scenario is the 40 per cent by which the equity market is assumed to fall.

Generally, the questions to assess the VaR figures are the same as those used for questioning the parameterisation of the model. The main difference is that, as a result of trying to determine a reasonably plausible extreme event, experts need to find a way to extrapolate the data available to infer the extreme events, for which little experience data is likely to exist to date. How this extrapolation is performed and the techniques that are and are not used are the key areas to challenge. The types of questions may include;

1. Why is the data set appropriate, relevant and sufficient? How did you come to that conclusion (what were the approaches and tests used)?
2. Why will the data remain an appropriate representation of future events?
3. What could make the data inappropriate?
4. What have you done to the data to come up with the potential stress tests? How has missing data been dealt with?
5. How have you extrapolated the data to create 'synthetic results' where the data is sparse (particularly at the extremes)?
6. What other approaches could have been used? What would the result be under these approaches? Why did you choose to reject these approaches?
7. What are the simplifications you have made? Why do they hold?
8. What are the elements of estimation and judgment?
9. What could occur to cause these simplifications, approximations and judgment to become inappropriate?

10. How are you monitoring the continued appropriateness of the simplifications, estimations and judgments?

When assessing risks, we are seeking to take a forward-looking view of an exposure. However, because the nature of the 'what if...?' scenarios on which VaR is assessed will, in the most part, be developed from historic data and not reflective of future evolutions or changes in the environment, VaR results will generally be an inaccurate or incomplete assessment of the risk exposure going forward.

For example, data used to assess credit default risk for financial institutions will be distorted by the credit crisis of 2008 and not reflect the changes in market practices and regulation that have occurred or are being proposed, such that if you are considering buying bank corporate debt to hold over the next ten years, the risk assessment will, most likely, reflect that this is a poor investment opportunity relative to other industries' corporate debt. As outlined earlier, this is because VaR tells you about a relative movement in riskiness since the previous day, not about the risk going forward. The measure has not taken account of any changes in approach to managing banks, which would need to be factored into any investment decision.

For regulatory reporting purposes, where the regulator is only looking at extreme adverse events over the coming year, these inaccuracies may not be too material. However, for business planning and projections of risk capital requirements many years into the future, judgment needs to be applied as to the likely continued appropriateness and evolution of risks over time. For simplicity, many companies continue to use the current 'what if...?' scenario in those future projections, and thus, the decision about relative value of opportunities becomes as much about, for example, companies taking the view that the relative value of buying the bank debt is low because the regulatory capital demands are high, irrespective of a longer-term view on whether this capital number is right going forward or not. It is very difficult to build a model that develops appropriate forward-looking adjustments to the data from the past such that a regulator would be comfortable adopting the approach for regulatory reporting purposes.

7.2.5.1   *Validating the internally assessed 'what if...?' scenarios*

Having developed the model and parameters from the data available, the output needs to be validated. We focus on four areas that are important in considering the appropriateness of the parameterisation of the 'what if...?' scenario:

(i) materiality of the risk
(ii) how the scenario has been applied
(iii) validation
(iv) expert judgment

(i) *Materiality of the risk.* Quantifying the materiality of the risk being considered ensures the importance of the implications is understood and a proportionate amount of focus is given to how the assessment has been carried out. The company should determine results relative to a set of materiality criteria. Aspects that could be considered in developing the materiality criteria include:

- the impact of a ± 20 per cent change in the underlying parameters
- pre or post the allowance for the benefit of diversification
- net or gross of hedging or reinsurance
- impact on new business pricing
- absolute or percentage increase in the capital requirement

Additionally, with materiality it is important to understand whether or not the net exposure is a result of a large notional and a small probability, and the speed with which the notional has accumulated. An error in a small probability applied to a large notional could result in a very large loss.
For example:

Example 7.1 : Example of a large notional and small probability
£10,000,000,000 × 0.1% = £10,000,000
£10,000,000,000 × 1% = £100,000,000

In many instances, an assessment of an extreme event calibrated by moving a small number by a large percentage does not amount to very much. In Example 7.1, applying a 50 per cent stress to the probability of 0.1 per cent would move the number to 0.15 per cent and the capital impact by £5m. However, with small probabilities, it may be appropriate to consider a minimum absolute movement or floor. In the above example, a minimum movement of 1 per cent would have given a materially different result to the headline-grabbing 50 per cent stress (the capital impact would have moved by some £90m). The appropriateness of establishing floors on stress tests needs to include an assessment of the volume and relevance of the underlying data in parameterising the base best estimate (in this example 0.1 per cent). The greater the certainty with the data, the less likely a floor is appropriate.

(ii) *Application of the 'what if...?' scenario.*   It is necessary to consider the manner of application of any proposed stress test and the nature of simplifications that may have been made in developing the calibration. This helps a company to understand whether the stress test may be inappropriate and unrepresentative of the risk exposure or when this breakdown in appropriateness may occur. For example,

– the 'what if...?' scenario may be applied as a percentage or absolute change in an assumption. As illustrated in Example 7.1, when the probability is small, a stress test based on a percentage change was not that onerous. There may be occasions in which a minimum absolute change is appropriate.
– the 'what if...?' scenario may be applied in the most onerous direction of stress at the individual policy level or the block of business level. Some stress tests may assume the change applies in the same direction across all blocks of business. However, this may not result in the most onerous impact on the capital position. For example, if the test assumes that persistence deteriorates across all products, it is possible that not all products will be adversely impacted by a deterioration because of surrender penalties or release of provisions for guarantees that no longer would be payable. Consideration needs to be given to the drivers of the risk event and whether a uniform application would be appropriate, or whether there is sufficient evidence to suggest that the application of a test in the most onerous direction would be more applicable.
– to control the number of 'what if...?' scenarios, sometimes simplifications are created to aggregate a stress test across a broad block of business. These simplifications may be in the form of implicit diversification between blocks of business or different subrisk categories (that is, a single test that is believed to cover both instantaneous changes in the parameter and any future changes resulting from a trend in experience). There is the risk that over time, a position builds up or is taken that arbitrages this simplification, which means the stress test is no longer appropriate. It is important to understand the reasons for choosing the level of granularity of the stress test that is used, what would cause this to be reviewed, and how this is being monitored.

(iii) *Validation.*   This is potentially the most important area for which a Board might provide challenge.

Management need to be able to provide an explanation of how statistical and other tests have been used to validate the data and derive the final proposal. The validation needs to cover the approach that was taken, what other approaches could have been used, and why they were not deemed appropriate.

A key part of the validation process is to put the results in a real-world context. For example, we find that the inclusion of some cause-based analysis to validate the results of the technical analysis is helpful, such as, a cause-based analysis of longevity risk may consider the impact of a cure for cancer. This approach helps convert a statistical result into something that the Board can feel able to tangibly relate to, and form a view as to the relative level of the extremeness of the test being proposed.

(iv) *Expert judgment.*   In finalising the 'what if…?' scenario, it is important to understand where expert judgment has been applied, the rationale for the expert judgment adopted, who applied the expert judgment, and why they are qualified as an expert. The explanation should include information relating to when the judgment will no longer be appropriate, and how this is being monitored so that the thinking and assumptions will be adjusted accordingly.

As the 'what if…?' scenarios will be based on the application of mathematics and not the real world, any approach will have limitations, constraints or areas for further development on which judgment has been applied, which needs to be made explicit. Understanding of the application of expert judgment not only provides an understanding of when the analysis breaks down, but also insight into the level of understanding by management of the model and its limitations. This insight will be useful in gaining comfort as to the level of authority to delegate, knowing that management understands how and when to apply judgment to the output from the model in its day-to-day decision-making.

Consider:

A director tried to establish regular updates with a CEO to explain assumptions, judgments and the reasons for movements in the financial position of his business over a certain period, prior to Board debates and approvals. The CEO did not want to meet and discuss these, and only wished to receive briefings as part of the Board meeting.

As a Board member, how much authority would you feel comfortable delegating to manage the business?

8
Structuring the Use of Risk Information

This chapter discusses ways of thinking about risk information and the use of risk registers. In particular, it will

– consider how risk registers can support the delegation of authority;
– consider an approach to enhancing engagement on operational risk issues;
– challenge the way we think about categorising risks.

8.1   Risk registers

The risk register can be one of the most important tools in helping a risk function engage in discussions about the management of the business. However, positioned incorrectly it can be one of the most disengaging and disregarded tools.

To make information output from the risk register useful, it needs to

– cover the totality of the risk landscape and link directly with performance information,
– help support how we want to think about, monitor and manage risks and performance internally, and
– ensure that what matters to the company remains firmly front and centre on the Board's radar.

8.1.1   Supporting the delegation of authority

The risk register can be used to evidence that management

– knows the risks facing the business,
– has controls in place,

– is taking actions where appropriate to strengthen its controls, and
– pre-emptively responds to threats and opportunities.

This evidence is the basis for giving the Board confidence that the level of authority and autonomy delegated to management remains appropriate. As such, the risk register needs to maintain sufficient details of the risks that are of concern to the management of the business and the delivery of its objectives, and in a way that provides evidence of a level of understanding of the opportunities and threats to the business.

Through the linkage of the performance metrics and the risk appetite dimensions, by considering events in the risk register against all risk appetite dimensions means that the 'level of concern' associated with each event can be aligned with the risk tolerances and thresholds agreed upon by the Board.

For example, we have experienced risk registers that simply articulate a risk as

yields rise and lead to an adverse deterioration of the balance sheet.

This articulation does not help identify the potential issues that may cause yields to rise, such that the key risk indicators, the controls that are in place, and the actions being taken to mitigate the risk can be clearly linked to the causes. Management needs to articulate the events,over the period being considered, that may trigger yields to rise. It is possible that the main concerns about what may cause yields to rise change over time, and hence, this is why the register should be regularly reviewed. Through maintaining this information management is evidencing an understanding of the business and market in which it operates, and ensures controls and key risk indicators are adapted to changing circumstances. In the above example, as the perception of a market recovery gains momentum, the fear may be that yields rise as investors divest from bonds and reinvest in equity markets linked to tapering of quantitative easing, whereas, at other times the fear may be that government debts are such that there is an increasing concern of government default.

The aim should be that information in the risk register, particularly for actions identified to rectify situations, is relevant, specific, measurable, owned, agreed upon and time-bound.

8.1.2 Supporting operational risk management

The origin of most risk registers is as a data collection system for operational risks. Over the years, these have become behemoths of data points relating to almost every risk and control. To many, the operational risk register has become a burden that is not actively updated and not used in support of the management of the business. The risk function needs to consider how to engage the business in a way that makes sense for the business and does not result in a pure data collection process, in which people become disengaged.

Key end users of the information are the business teams and the audit function. The business teams perform processes to deliver an end product. These processes involve people having access to information and systems, and the production of items that are checked and used by internal and external parties, such as the executive team, the Board, regulators and shareholders. Each of these processes has a potential for an adverse outcome based on the behaviours of people or failures in the process or systems. These potential adverse outcomes, when measured against the risk appetite dimensions, assist in understanding the processes we operate that could take us outside acceptable bounds of the risk appetite dimensions and thus give rise to a significant 'level of concern'.[1]

The operational risk assessment can be developed through producing a mapping of these processes and the key control points. At each key control point, the following questions need to be asked:

- What are the risks that need to be mitigated?
- How do the checks mitigate the risks?

In this process, redundant checks should be removed, and any areas of weaknesses assessed as to whether the benefits[2] of introducing/enhancing checks outweigh the costs.

Many financial reporting processes have been reviewed and challenged in this way in recent process improvement projects.In these projects, the checks and controls have been challenged to understand their purpose from a risk mitigation perspective, with much of the work having to do with understanding the potential materiality of errors and whether these would be of concern. In many cases, checks had evolved in processes to cover errors that had little impact on the end result, but they were making processes significantly inefficient and labour intensive.

The outcomes for the business of supporting the population of a risk system with a mapping of key business processes include the following:

1. The risk register provides a tool that is of use to the management of the business process, evidencing that key control checkpoints have been embedded.

2. The risk register is regularly reviewed and maintained through post-process reviews to capture process and control enhancements, with any actual loss events or near misses. This review and updating is done in a timely manner.

3. Understanding the implications of failures in the controls against the risk appetite dimensions assists audit in prioritising its annual review plans towards processes and controls that have the most material impact on the business and the delivery of its plan. This helps the business understand the rationale behind the audit plans.

4. Audit recommendations can be made that clearly articulate the benefit to the organisation of the business's committing time and resource to implementing additional controls or rectifying ineffective ones through an understanding of the benefit to the residual risk exposure against the cost of doing so.

A risk data capture template is shown in appendix E.

8.2   Structuring risk thinking

Much effort has been put into the categorisation of risk. However, the main driver for this has been to develop a framework that supports data analysis to strengthen the justifications for the amount of capital being held in the buffer, and comparisons of the profile of risk exposures with peer groups rather than as a facilitator of management discussion. For example, as the motor underwriting cycle softens and brokers stop placing business with a company, the focus of management is on corrective actions rather than identification of the most appropriate risk category into which to allocate the issues.

One approach to risk thinking that has been useful is the positioning of categories in terms of the nature of the action being considered in response to an event occurring. The risk landscape can be thought of as reflecting the risks, present or emerging, to the value of the company (enterprise value), which was illustrated in Section 4.2.

Enterprise value = value of net assets + the present value of the expected transfer to shareholders from in-force business + Goodwill

With the components of the enterprise value in mind, the following structure has been useful in supporting our thinking about how we identify, manage and respond to threats and opportunities:

1. tactical and operational risks (things over which we choose a tactical position)
2. strategy risks (things that may impact our strategic position)
3. emerging risks (things that are material in size and could become relevant to our tactical or strategic positioning in time)

8.2.1   Tactical and operational risks

Tactical and operational risks relate to managing the value of the company's net assets and the value of the profits that are expected to arise from of its in-force business[3].

Tactical risk management is about making decisions regarding an exposure which we are choosing to take in the short term because of the perceived potential benefit, and that we have the ability to change should we need to control the exposure to remain within a risk limit framework. An example of this is the upside from investing in risky assets, coupled with the ability to take actions such as responding to market risk events through the use of hedging strategies.

Operational risks can be thought of as the risks that arise from within the organisation that could be prevented. However, companies do not and cannot have a 'zero tolerance' for these risks as this would only be achieved by exiting the industry sector. These risks occur as a result of choosing to be 'in business', and companies, regulators and auditors need to understand, accept and tolerate that some errors or issues will arise because the costs associated with mitigating them is too high relative to the benefit. The way in which decisions are made about adding additional controls to mitigate these risks further is through standard cost-benefit analysis. When the cost of implementing mitigants exceeds the benefits of doing so, the organisation and shareholders may need to accept the level of risk.

8.2.2   Strategy risk

Strategy risk relates to managing the value of goodwill.

Strategy risk focuses on developing responses to events that have implications for the future strategy of the company. For example, a concern over a ratcheting exposure to equity risk changing the risk profile over the business planning horizon could be managed by changing a feature in the product design for new business or changing the pricing approach to cover the explicit cost of buying appropriate hedging instruments, all of which may impact the value of goodwill. These actions are different from a tactical response, such as hedging the equity risk on the current exposure.

8.2.3   Emerging risks

Emerging risks are newly developing or changing risks which are difficult to quantify and may have a major impact on the organisation and the ability to realise thegoodwill over the plan horizon.Emerging risks canbe thought of as events that canmigrate to becoming material concerns for the organisation, which need to be monitored and responses to which need to be proactively considered. Anexample would be a risk that is presently beyond the required likelihood for assessment under the economic capital framework, but is evolving fast and may impact the enterprise value in the future.

Emerging risk management needs to address the concern that we cannot manage what we donot know. The risk category is widely accepted as existingseparate from other risk categories, because the way of thinking about these risks evolving needs to be allowed to diverge from the structured approaches that underpin other risk assessments. This is because these events may emerge from paths of evolution that have not been seen yet.

> *If you did not know, why would you think a caterpillar would emerge from a cocoon with wings?*

Emerging risk analysis is most usefully extended to understand the nature of opportunities that may also arise after an event has emerged. This enables companies to think about how best to respond to current events in a way that enables them to position themselves to take advantage of these opportunities. Through the credit crisis of 2008, much of the analysis was limited to focussing on the downsides of the crisis, without considering the potential opportunities that would be created as, for example, institutions withdrew from markets, or economies tried to recover and new investors were required to kick-start growth. Hence, many companies were slow to react as opportunities presented themselves.

9
Risk Culture

This chapter provides coverage of the drivers of risk culture and how to identify strengths and weaknesses. In particular, it will show

– the influences on risk culture,
– how risk culture can be evolved,
– signs of strength and weakness in risk culture,
– how to challenge the risk culture to ensure hot spots are managed.

9.1   Questions for the Board

Establishing a culture is about motivating the right behaviours. The support and engagement of the Board is critical in creating the right risk culture. The strongest signal a Board provides is in the recruitment of the chief executive officer (CEO). The attitude and approach of the CEO and his or her chosen executive team will set the perceptions and create the behaviours others will look to emulate. When seeking to understand and influence the culture of the company, the Board should ask where the company exhibits perceived strengths and weaknesses in its culture, as outlined in Section 9.6, and consider how to monitor hot spots that might cause the risk culture to decline in effectiveness, as discussed in Section 9.7.

9.2   Background to risk culture

Harrison (1972), Handy (1976), Peters and Waterman (1982), and Kotter and Heskett proposed that successful companies (those that significantly outperform others) have strong coherent cultures. The Bath University/

CIPD report 'Unlocking the black box' reaffirmed that the link between strategy and performance is culture.

In an international survey reported in Farrell and Hoon (2009), 48 per cent of 500 bank executives who participated cited a deficient risk culture as a leading contributor to the credit crisis. As companies looked for return in benign markets, the cultures created an attitude of denial about the true underlying risks and their potential impacts.

But what *is* a risk culture?

The complexity of a risk culture is that it is based on motivating a set of behaviours that are influenced by an individual's ambitions, perceptions and emotions, which can appear irrational and illogical at times.

An ex-colleague could not decipher why managers behaved and responded to events differently from him. The difference lay in the personal conflicts between values and ambition – in difficult circumstances, some individuals will not compromise values for the sake of ambition, while others will put ambitions ahead of values.

Culture is the combination of behaviours of people in the organisation that drives the way decisions are taken at all levels in the organisation.

Developing a picture of the behaviours that we want is very straightforward. However, embedding these behaviours in the 'unconscious competent' responses of employees is extremely difficult. This is the challenge in creating and sustaining a good culture: taking employees on a journey from 'unconscious incompetence' through the stages of learning and adaption to 'unconscious competence'. Simply stated, the stages of learning and adaptation take an individual from

- learning about what is being done as part of a norm of behaviour that is inappropriate (unconscious incompetence), through
- conscious recognition and attempts to adapt the behaviours, to
- competently doing the right thing, but having to continue to think about it to make it happen, to finally
- doing the right thing without having to think about it (unconscious competence).

Think back to learning about how to drive a car. To begin with, you probably thought you could drive but did not really understand or accept that this was not the case. Having started to take lessons, you were not very good at driving and really had to think about everything you did to get it right. Eventually, you reached a level of competence at which you drove correctly without having to think about everything in detail.

Cultural change projects can create a framework and sense of direction, but employees will need to see evidence of any new approach being supported before they start to learn and adapt their behaviours. This process of learning and adapting is why embedding a good risk culture is an extremely difficult and long process.

9.3   Defining risk culture

A risk culture manifests itself through the way things get done, that is, how employees behave in identifying, understanding and acting on the risks the organisation confronts on a day-to-day basis. The sign of a good risk culture is that the sense of responding by 'doing the right thing' is valued and encouraged more than 'doing whatever it takes to get on'.

If we imagine that the formalised set of rules and procedures provides a box or framework within which to operate, culture is the social and less cognitive aspect that determines how people play and create chaos in the spaces within these formal boundaries – the space between the rules.

Writing a code of ethics or going through a process to define the space within which people should behave and make decisions is easy, but it can be just words on a page unless this is backed up by non-verbal methods of communication from management, to which employees pay far more attention. Consider the verbal and non-verbal messages from Enron. The Enron Code of Ethics (July 2000) stated:

> Employees are charged with conducting their business affairs in accordance with the highest ethical standards. An employee shall not conduct himself or herself in a manner which directly or indirectly would be detrimental to the best interests of the company or in a manner which would bring the employee financial gain separately derived as a direct consequence of his or her employment with the company.

By the end of 2001, Enron went from a $100bn revenue business to bankruptcy, with numerous of its executives charged with criminal acts, including fraud and insider trading. Rather than creating real value, management's goal was 'keeping up appearances' and maintaining a rising stock price, backed by a culture of reward for results at any price.

9.4   Influencing the development of the risk culture

The key influence to the culture of an organisation comes from the top because staff will reflect the signals they receive from their leaders in order

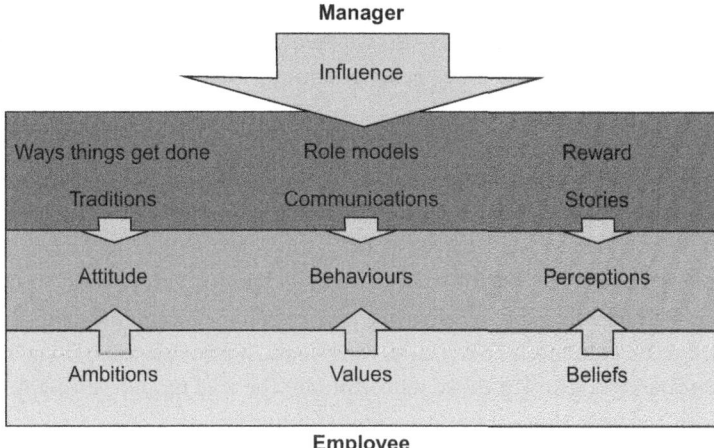

Figure 9.1   Influencing the development of culture

to secure and advance their ambitions. However, the personal beliefs and values of staff that underpin culture cannot be changed by senior management directly; management must rely on influence and example to change the way in which the culture manifests itself. This means that staff need to experience events and scenarios that reinforce the changes in culture that are required, which can mean as much about evidencing that inappropriate behaviours are not tolerated and dealt with.

Figure 9.1 illustrates the interactions between personal attributes and the environment that can influence the establishment of the risk culture.

Each employee has a set of core values, beliefs and ambitions, whether these are dominated by integrity and security, or money and position. These impact employees' employee's attitudes, behaviours and perceptions towards the working environment. Equally, aspects of the working environment impact employees' attitudes, behaviours and perceptions. Management need to recruit those individuals who possess the preferred values, beliefs and ambitions and seek to evidence that the working environment mutually reinforces their attitudes, behaviours and perceptions. Issues arise when these aspects of influence create frictions at the interface between the working environment and employees' attitudes, behaviours and perceptions. These frictions can manifest themselves in increased staff turnover rates or business inefficiencies.

Motivating changes in employees' attitudes, behaviours and perceptions requires investment in demonstrating what the company values, through

1. leaders as role models – how do we show what is acceptable behaviour?
2. recognition and reward – how do we evidence what we value most?
3. working environment – how do we encourage the right ways to get things done?

Section 9.4.1 outlines the issues associated with each of these dimensions, which are later addressed in Section 9.5.

9.4.1 Leaders as role models

Shaping behaviours is about creating role models whose values and beliefs we want to be emulated. This means that we must also reinforce this perception through recognising those who emulate the role models, and applying sanctions to those that do not meet our standards.

9.4.1.1 *Human drivers of culture and ethics*

> No matter how wonderful your governance processes, if you cannot trust your people, then you are at risk – Sir Derek Higgs

Boards make decisions based on whether what is being proposed is possible[1] to do, profitable, and also whether it is aligned with their principles.

When markets have been tough, regularly the term 'being commercial' is misused to excuse those to answer comfortably the question of alignment with principles. This plays to the core of culture-

Evidence the answer to the question 'Are principles as important to you as profit?'

There are many examples of situations in which principles, ethics or doing what is right have been difficult questions to face. It is not that an individual's actions have been illegal, but it is about signalling principles that matter to the company. In the longer term, it may be that the benefits of facing the reality of the third question related to principles, and not just doing whatever it takes, is more 'commercial' than avoiding it.

The term commercial is about knowing how to use the entirety of the space between the rules afforded for the culture and not a small subsection of the area within the formal boundaries.

Consider the following examples:

1. In the United States, leading up to 2007, to keep pace with their peers in the market, banks shortcut affordability checks on the sale of loans to those who they knew would have difficulty meeting repayments.
2. To support bank expansion plans, there was widespread issuing of credit cards to those whose ability to manage debt and meet repayments would

be challenging. Do banks have a responsibility to those to whom they lend?

3. In 2012–2013, Google, Amazon, Apple and Starbuck's were questioned about the very low levels of tax they paid. Their actions were not illegal, but were their actions in the interest of all stakeholders? How was the balance determined? Who ends up paying?

4. In the UK, parliamentary privilege has been used to disclose the names of individuals to whom the Courts had granted anonymity.

5. There have been issues raised about mis-selling of payment protection insurance and wholesale gas pricing.

In presenting these examples, we are not concluding that the end result in all cases should have been different on ethical and commercial grounds, but rather we are highlighting that the issues are not always straightforward. Would companies respond by saying that, in many instances, they are a reflection of customer and shareholder short-termism, ethics and principles? Would customers and shareholders take their business elsewhere if managers did not do what they do, that is, managers could not they create the long term without managing the short term?

An individual's drivers of cultural and ethical behaviour are shaped by his or her personal integrity, social conscience, and regard for rules and laws.

Regard for rules and laws.   Rules and laws provide us with guidance as to the boundaries of behaviour that is acceptable. It should be noted that this does not mean that all rules and laws are fair.

Establishing these boundaries is particularly important when there are individuals whose personal integrity, or attitude toward society more widely, is less well developed such that it is difficult for them to discern appropriate acceptable behaviours. As these individuals tend to look for ways to change the boundaries by trying to bend the rules or find new areas to which the rules do not apply, there is the tendency for the rules and policies to multiply. This is because the rules and policies are used as a way of controlling an outcome, rather than dealing with the root cause of the problem – recruiting people with the right behaviours and values at outset.

The proliferation of rules and policies can cause a drag on company performance:

– Rules and policies can be costly to maintain and police, but it is important to ensure they are enforced to signal the boundaries of acceptable behaviour.

- As the consequences of rule-breaking need to be enforced to make rules effective, staff can become reticent about taking actions for fear of breaching a complex set of rules.
- Rules and policies take the onus away from an individual to behave in an appropriate manner and may lead to game playing on the margins around the rules and policies. The actions and behaviours may not breach the current rules, but result in an increase in the number of rules, and the tightening of existing ones to the detriment of the organisation. This can stifle the creativity of staff, the development of a learning culture, and embed a perception that management mistrust staff.

The danger of a framework based on rules and policies is that it can lead, for those more guided by ethical principles, to a sense of 'obey or be punished'. In order to avoid this working environment becoming embedded, it is important to regularly remove individuals who might drive this moral decline and promote those who advance a more 'adult' working environment.

Social conscience.   Social conscience is a sense that people have regarding the consequences of their actions on others. They will base their behaviours on what will benefit the majority of people. Within an organisation, such employees will consider the implications of their actions on those with whom they interact, both internal and external to the organisation. This attribute can prevent siloed thinking and encourage the delivery of actions that are in the best interests of the wider Group.

Personal integrity.   Personal integrity is central to defining our own character, how we control our behaviours and make what we believe to be rational decisions. Personal integrity is the element that brings dealing with the truth into conflict with managing personal ambition, and is the reason why a great number of people find it hard to do the right thing. Behaving with integrity requires the greatest amount of courage, as it means we have to stand up to others to do what is right and admit when we have done something wrong.

Research has suggested that a person develops a sense of integrity from a number of values such as intellect, fairness, courage, humility and honesty. Behaving with integrity does not mean that he or she practices these values to extreme. Extremely open and honesty disclosures can be overtly brutal, for example, to those who receive the message, and courage in extreme can manifest itself as a stubborn response that is equally unhelpful. Thus, there is a balance between not having enough integrity and going too far to uphold it.

Research by James C Collins has supported these values as central to high-performing companies. In *Good to great: why some companies make the leap and others don't* (2001), he describes how leaders with moral values such as humility, courage, self-control and passion are at the core of long-term highly successful cultures. This was based on his analysis of over 1,400 companies. In *How the mighty fall: and why some companies never give in* (2009), he shows conversely that cultures dominated by ego, greed and fear destroy businesses.

This research highlights the importance of ensuring that an organisation embeds the right sort of culture.

Establishing the right culture requires a core team with the appropriate set of values and a suitable approach to ethical behaviour. This team needs to operate in an environment that is not overtly controlled by rules and policies. Too many rules will stifle creativity and disengage people from utilising their core values and acting with humility, courage, self-control and passion. The aim must be to create an environment in which individuals use their own values as a basis for their decision-making.

If you want an ethical culture, you need ethical leaders.

9.4.1.2 *Power structure*

The power structure of an organisation can have a significant influence on employees' behaviours, and it is usually an unspoken operating model that drives the dynamics of the risk culture. Within most organisations, the CEO has 'a right-hand person'. This individual is usually easily identified by staff working within the organisation who analyse decisions taken by senior management that relate to organisational design, allocation of budget and reward. From this, staff members determine the key individuals within the organisation whom they need to support, and whose style and behaviour they need to emulate to further their careers or secure continued employment.

The creation of an environment that is supported by social silences serves to maintain a power structure. Employees who feel unable to challenge strategies can be an important indicator of the emergence of an 'untouchable executive' or a 'self-interested silo' within the organisation, and should be a red flag to a risk committee and a Board.

As an example, Siemens is a large German engineering company. In 2006, a regulatory investigation found that a large number of employees were paying millions of euros into funds and shell companies established to win contracts and pay bribes. As a new CEO came in to move the business forwards, both internal and external investigations were instigated.

However, they found some internal resistance to disclosing information remained, until an amnesty for whistle-blowers (excluding directors) was announced following which a large number came forward with incriminating evidence.

One of the signs of a good risk culture is the ability and willingness of employees to openly challenge what appear to be significant areas of growth, profitability and return. This will only happen if it is led by a CEO who asks the difficult questions and explodes the myth of 'unchallengeable relationships'.

In 2011, a Group's independent assurance function planned a deep dive review of the pricing of a key product in one of its units following concerns over its profitability. Prior to the review commencing, the local finance team, which also had responsibility for the pricing, produced its own reportedly 'independent' deep dive report that suggested all was okay. This was a big red flag to the organisation's risk committee, not only about the conflicts within the local finance team but the approach of members of the senior management team who appeared to support the avoidance of an independent review.

In 2013, an external consultancy was hired to undertake a review of the approach to pricing the key product in the unit, as the Group's balance sheet had continued to decline.

9.4.1.3 Leadership style

The attitude and actions of the Board and senior management will be reflected in the behaviour of staff. Staff will seek to emulate those at the top, as reflecting their approach and attitude will be perceived as that which the company requires in order for an individual to get on. Any contradictions between what is written down and what is enacted will result in staff following actions rather than words.

A company had a policy that all employees had to transfer between buildings using the footbridge and not run across a dangerous road that separated them. However, the CEO was continually seen by staff running across the road between the corporate buildings rather than using the footbridge as outlined in the policy. The CEO was never reprimanded. The rule was never enforced more widely and became redundant.

Managers need to demonstrate the values of the company in the way in which they make decisions, and ensure that any policies and rules are ones that they feel appropriately subject to, and that the sanctions are proportionate should the sanctions need to be applied to them.

How leaders manage significant events. Generally, people's first reaction to an adverse event is to experience a state of shock or denial. Once the reality of the situation starts to hit home, people tend to react negatively with anger and fear, actively resisting the consequences of what has happened. This reaction can be driven by a genuine understanding of the threats to their position or by misestimating the consequences. Management's role is to move through these emotional states as quickly as possible to arrive at a position in which solutions can be advanced and the business can move forward again.

How management reacts to significant events has to do with minimising the negative impact of what happens and helping people adapt quickly to their new environment. Management need to engender an approach focussed on outcomes rather than fear and blame.

During the strategic planning process, a three- or five-year plan will be developed, along with a more detailed one-year plan for the coming year. These plans make a number of assumptions about what is expected to happen over the coming years. In delivering the annual plan, there may be incidents that lead to deviations from the assumptions in the plan. Some of these deviations may be significant and material, such as significant financial market fluctuations which change the available financial capacity to take on new business and operate securely. The way in which management responds to this, and the attention, priority and leadership they provide to the delivery of the solution will provide staff with physical evidence of the importance of risk management to the organisation. If management remains in denial about risks, staff will learn not to flag issues, which may lead dangerously to apathy.

As many financial institutions learned to their detriment in the financial crisis of 2008, the leadership style adopted by senior management in times of continuous outperformance is as important as that in periods of extreme stress. The most difficult time to hear bad news is when business is booming. These are the times when being open to challenge and acting on seemingly counterintuitive opinions test our courage, integrity and ethical values.

9.4.1.4 *Leadership of a learning culture*

A critical aspect of a good risk culture is one that does not get caught in denial or fear, but can accept that mistakes happen and errors occur as part of being in a state of continuous improvement. Following correction to a risk limit breach, it is a sign of a good culture to be able to investigate how the breach can be prevented from recurring. The feedback loop needs to embed a feeling that it is not about finding fault but finding a better operational space. Management style is critical to the way in which employees engage with the feedback process. Tolerating errors of judgment, but not errors of principle, is imperative.

9.4.2   Recognition and reward

Incentive schemes, performance targets and management information influence the way in which we behave and what we focus our attention on. It is not just about the financial rewards but the perception we create of the criteria by which we recruit, reward, promote and exit members of staff.

Throughout the late 1990s, CUC International established a track record of delivering on aggressive revenue growth targets. Yet following a merger, the results were found to be fraudulent. Employees disclosed to investigators that they had felt pressured by management to adjust accounting records to meet expectations.

9.4.2.1   Financial reward

Companies need to evolve an approach to compensation that encourages decisions to be made in the best interests of the wider Group rather than embed a siloed, self-interested mentality within business units.

Consider: A strategic consultancy operates a reward system in which each partner's bonus is directly linked to the value of the contracts he or she wins. This practice drives each partner to secure his or her own client base, reduce information sharing and deliver without engaging other partners unless absolutely necessary. The risks of this approach include clients receiving multiple contacts from the company and solutions that are suboptimal, thus reducing both the credibility and long-term revenue of the consultancy.

During the pre-financial market turmoil of 2008, many approaches to financial reward appeared to balance revenue and risk-taking[2]. However, when it came to the crunch, executives reinforced the picture that revenue was the main consideration as they strove to report important market metrics at consistent levels with peers that were perceived to be drivers of share price growth and the value of their bonuses.

9.4.2.2   Developing and promoting role models

Staff will look at what it takes to further their career as a gauge of what behaviours and values are needed and desired within the organisation.

Following a number of crises, including the LIBOR rate-fixing scandal, and questions about its culture, Barclays made a number of new appointments in 2012–2013. While there were new messages about Barclays's approach, there were also some messages in the backgrounds of individuals appointed to senior roles. For example,

- Sir David Walker (Chairman) previously had led a government enquiry into how banks were run;
- Sir Hector Sants (Head of Compliance) was previously CEO at the UK financial services regulator.

People look for evidence of what will help them get on in a company and signs of what might hinder their ambitions. One area that is a strong signal for this is the attributes of those who are promoted. Nearly all announcements about promotions focus on what the individual has achieved and brings to the table, with the stark absence of comments on their values and behaviours. This is an area in which we may see more balance going forward.

Staff appraise the attributes of individuals who are recruited or promoted, and draw conclusions as to how they need to adapt their behaviour to get on.

Thus, managers need to promote individuals who have both the talent and core values to enhance the desired culture, as these individuals will be assessed as role models of the company's requirements. Understanding an individual's core values, communicating company expectations and assessing his or her fit, is an essential part the interview process, as having to exit a 'role model' with the wrong cultural attributes can be a time-consuming and costly process. For example, a manager who is singularly career minded will surround him- or herself with a team who are equally willing to 'do whatever it takes' to secure their own future progression, which can mean that exiting the manager for poor cultural fit will require that the team leaders must be exited as well.

There is the example of a finance director (FD) who did not bid for any project budget within the planning cycle, despite his management team requesting many millions of dollars for projects they needed to pursue to meet his objectives. In the first quarter, the project proposals came in with demands for budget. As these were priority projects for finance, the FD approved the spend for the projects to go ahead and informed his management he would confirm with the CEO the 'pots' from which budget would be drawn.

During the second quarter's business plan reforecasting process, the project costs came to light, the finance function was significantly over budget, and it was clear the CEO was not fully briefed on the project budget requirements.

The FD quickly blamed his managers and project managers for not controlling budget and being over ambitious. A number of these individuals were exited from the business. The finance management team, now aware of the culture that the FD operated, adjusted their approach to gaining approvals and visibility with the CEO. Most recently, the CEO has appointed a direct report to manage all projects and communications to ease his increased workload. The outcome of this cultural approach has been to increase the timescales for approval, cost and bureaucracy.

9.4.2.3   Perceived objective performance measures

Employees look for signals of what is important to the senior management of the organisation. One of the strongest signals is what management pay attention to and measure, which can provide an objective basis against which performance and the delivery of value can be evaluated.

Hence, if information about the risks and the impact of the risks being taken is not actively measured and monitored by management, its importance will be denigrated, as management will be perceived to be disinterested. Excessive delegation of authority or reporting of risk by exception will provide staff with the perception that this is actually not important. Reporting risks by exception is regularly viewed as a sign that management is not overtly concerned about this aspect of risk management, and as a result, a rigorous approach to the identification and assessment of risk can prove difficult to embed, with actions to correct risk exposures not happening in a timely manner.

Checks and control failures are also visible and measurable performance outcomes. Employees will commit more time and effort to areas in which checks and controls exist because any failings will appear on management's radar.

9.4.2.4   Linking the business strategy to operational targets

If employees can see a direct link between what they do day to day and how that supports the delivery of the strategic vision of the organisation, then they can buy-in to channelling their passion to deliver for the organisation.

Can your people do the elevator pitch, without using jargon or corporate speak, to explain what the organisation is trying to achieve, how their role helps deliver it, and what the purpose is of any boundaries within which they are required to operate?

To do this requires a clear and concise articulation of the strategy and performance objectives, which are the links to the operational boundaries for exposures to risks that transparently align with controlling the delivery of activities that constitute the day-to-day management of the business.

9.4.3 Working environment

9.4.3.1 Enforcement of rules and policies

Rules and policies outlining expected levels of ethical behaviour and competence need to be backed up by appropriate remedial actions when they are breached.

Inaction against breaches of policies, such as not taking appropriate action against a member of staff whose behaviours are not consistent with the values of the organisation, informs others in the organisation as to the actual acceptable expectations. It becomes easier for employees to breach policies without fear of sanctions when policies are not implemented consistently between senior and junior employees and by different departments within the organisation. The approach and application of sanctions for breach of a policy is equally as important as the policy itself.

Assessing and supporting developmental needs

For all its various roles, an organisation needs to specify the required levels of knowledge and skill required to perform the roles and ensure that these are reflected in role profiles, and that the appropriate framework for training and development is in place. Employees will infer whether risk management is important to the organisation from the requirements within the role profiles and the supporting commitment to training and developing the skills needed to discharge their duties outlined in these role profiles. Competency requirements outlined in role profiles without the support of adequate training will be deemed unnecessary.

Is your approach to risk and compliance training a 10-question Internet game?

9.4.3.2 Communication and information sharing

An organisation provides both internal and external communications, which can influence employees' attitude and behaviours. Employees will read external communications, with any inconsistency between internal messages and external communications creating perceptions about management's attitudes and values[3].

The attitude of management towards receiving feedback from external stakeholders will create perceptions about the importance attached to these groups. For example, managements' approach to dealing with customer complaints and using their feedback to identify opportunities to enhance the business proposition will send strong messages about the value attached to the customer experience.

Informal communication channels are at least as important as formal channels. They provide an opportunity to extract information that otherwise would not be forthcoming in formal channels because of fear of expressing bad news officially. Strong networks that enable employees to feel comfortable engaging with the risk function about emerging concerns ensures issues can be dealt with quickly before they become more serious problems.

For example, a potential fraud was discovered at a company following a ten-minute chat over coffee between an accountant and an actuary. The accountant bemoaned the size of some expense payments being made to a company owned by an ex-employee for work done on behalf of a current director. When the next expense analysis was produced, the actuary investigated further. The potential exposure was around £20m, the case was settled out of court, and the director involved was removed from office.

With forms of electronic communication such as email, blogging and tweeting, additional consideration needs to be given to the tone of the communication, as scope exists to more easily misinterpret the intent of a message resulting in acrimonious exchanges that could easily have been avoided. Additionally, conversing in manners other than face to face can create a sense of detachment or lack of ownership for the issue or risk being discussed. This is why paying for goods and services by credit card is more risky than paying by cash. With credit cards, there is a detachment from the medium of exchange. Having £50 in your wallet and watching it being used over a week is a more tangible approach to expense control than expenditure on 'plastic'.

The more management is seen to walk the floor and engage with staff as people, the more likely staff are to be willing and able to engage about issues and concerns. A faceless senior manager is someone with whom people are more likely to take on an attitude of 'I'm not too bothered about flagging this, given the extra pain it could cause me'. Conversely, few people wish to see colleagues whom they know and respect lose their job over something they could have forewarned them about.

The objective of a risk function is to prevent communications from becoming a one-way flow of information by creating opportunities to draw out conversations about uncertainties and how to manage them.

9.4.3.3 Subcultures

Whatever culture a Group wishes to implement, business units, national boundaries and mergers and acquisitions will give rise to subcultures within an organisation. The danger of these subcultures is that they represent the power base of local executives who see their unit as a silo and not as part of the bigger Group. Strong performing units can perceive what they do as better than that undertaken across the wider Group. These units can be difficult entities with which to embed Group-wide metrics, information or policy, as they see these as impositions on the operation of their business that 'knows how to deliver value'. Equally, underperforming units that are concerned about being sold off can be difficult places from which to extract quality, accurate information. Both these types of units benefit from having staff seconded from Group into the unit and vice versa, to give each an understanding of the other's reasons for requiring information and for the opportunity to remove 'faceless interaction' going forward, thus making it harder to be obstinate and providing an opportunity to understand the reality of the situation within a business unit.

A global bank acquired a Mexican operation. Members of the Mexican management team were posted around the new Group. In 2012, the Group chief risk officer (CRO) discovered a trail of controls that did not meet Group standards at entities where these staff members were posted. The former Mexican management team had had a different attitude towards controls over checking sources of funds being deposited from those established by the multinational group that had acquired them. At the end of 2012, the Group was fined heavily by the US regulators for its money-laundering controls.

Challenge from a Board on mergers and acquisitions should not only be about whether the benefits are reasonable and achievable, but also how the integration of people and processes is going to tangibly deliver these benefits. If you are buying a business because of its growth potential or market access, cultural friction could cause key personnel to leave the business and the acquirer to be left with the proverbial 'lemon', or conversely, the acquirer could be infected by the acquired company's culture and suffer financial, brand and reputational damage.

9.4.3.4 *Organisational systems and procedures*

The approach to managing systems and procedures gives staff an indication of the importance and attitude of the organisation towards the controls that are in operation. A continuous improvement ethos is useful at challenging the 'we've always done it this way' mentality and prevents apathy about risks occurring as people review and challenge the implications of what they do, and how they do it.

9.4.3.5 *Delegation of authority*

To function effectively, authority to make decisions needs to be cascaded down through each level of an organisation in a way that empowers employees to use their knowledge and experience to respond to business issues quickly and efficiently. However, delegating too many decisions and too much authority such that senior management see and confirm few decisions can be perceived as management becoming disinterested in decision-making and risks in that area. A side effect of this approach is that management see themselves as immune from responsibility if others make decisions that go wrong, rather than accepting responsibility and ensuring that the process and delegation of authority are appropriate.

In 2012, the British Broadcasting Corporation (BBC) launched an investigation into historic allegations of inappropriate behaviour against Sir Jimmy Savile, only for it to be axed by executives before it was aired.

Following many interviews, enquiries, claims and counterclaims over who knew what and who made decisions, a number of high-profile directors at the BBC resigned or were removed from office, including the recently appointed director general, George Entwistle.

The sense was that the framework for decision-making was such that Entwistle and others should have been engaged more in the decisions about the programme being aired given the nature of the investigation, and the potential for damage to the public's 'trust' of the BBC.

9.5 Evolving the right culture

Section 9.4 highlighted the areas that influence the risk culture. Section 9.5 outlines how these areas can be developed to evolve and support the right culture.

9.5.1 Leaders as role models

Many organisations start by establishing a Group-wide set of common values and providing a framework for rewarding individuals who provide examples of what 'living the values' means. This framework needs to ensure that the reward for living the values is as great as for 'delivering the outcome'.

The recruitment process is critical to ensuring that those who do *not* fit with the desired behaviours of the organisation are filtered out prior to joining. The interview process provides the first impressions of the organisation and needs to transmit a message to the prospective candidate about the organisation's values, culture and operating style. This is a key point in communicating the desired behaviours and values to the candidate and assessing his or her 'goodness of fit'. When the new employee first joins the organisation, the importance of the company's values and culture should be emphasised by senior management during any new employee orientation.

The performance review process should include behavioural dimensions to ensure that this 'goodness of fit' is reassessed on an annual basis and that those who have inappropriate behaviours are provided with development and coaching plans, or are dealt with accordingly.

The recruitment of an individual who does not believe in the company values, or is misaligned, can send a strong message to staff about the real attitude of the company towards the culture and values. Aligning these at the recruitment stage is as important as getting the appropriate intellectual fit. Misalignment can lead to turnover of staff who have a positive cultural fit and to an undermining of the long-term embedding of desired behaviours, as individuals tend to recruit staff with the same values.

Consider the footballing era at Manchester United under Alex Ferguson and Roy Keane. There are many photographs of Ferguson's robust approaches to match officials and of the Manchester United players surrounding and lambasting referees.

Is the behaviour of teams on the pitch a reflection of what is accepted off the field of play and of the cultural expectations?

This 'tone from the top' can be monitored through the annual staff survey and exit interviews.

9.5.2   Recognition and reward

The system of performance incentives needs to balance a number of competing dimensions that include the performance objectives as well an assessment of risk management.

A key enabler for the performance appraisal framework is the development of risk-based management information that is useable at the front line and can be aggregated up through the organisation to the Board, evidencing how the delivery of the strategy and objectives is being managed. This approach ensures that what is being measured for performance purposes drives behaviours and decisions that are consistent with and appropriate for the organisation's aims.

Recent evolutions of performance assessment frameworks include measures associated with risk responsiveness, collaboration, stakeholder satisfaction, compliance with risk policies, appetite and limits, and ability to listen and be challenged. Performance assessment is an area in which 360 feedback and specific sections from staff engagement surveys can provide useful inputs to these subjective components of the bonus calculation.

With respect to measurement and reward, the areas that are particularly important to consider include

- an objective performance and promotion framework that balances the recognition of performance and behaviours;
- review of areas that continuously 'outperform' when others continuously 'perform' in order to ensure that the objectives and targets that are used for performance management purposes are equally challenging and achievable.

It is important for staff to see the behaviours that are being encouraged and that those individuals who do not meet the required standard are incentivised to change and not encouraged to continue their behaviour unabated. This message will be most evident in the financial incentive schemes in which the importance of behaviours will be seen to be measured alongside the objectives delivered.

From the strategic planning process, the goals of the organisation should be clearly articulated, balance risk and reward, and cascade through departmental objectives and performance targets, into individuals' objectives and performance targets. This means that one of the outcomes should be that an individual's operational targets, that are used day to day on the front line, should clearly link to the risk policies and risk tolerances agreed upon within the strategic plan, in order to ensure that employees understand the importance of how the organisation manages risk and the implications for delivering the organisation's objectives.

9.5.2   Working environment

The evolution of a strong risk culture is supported by a working environment in which an influential CRO is part of the executive team, symbolising the importance of risk management.

To build the trust of staff, internal and external communications from senior management need to be aligned, providing a clear and consistent message. One of the most important internal communications is the transparency with which budgets, resources and targets have been established from the strategic planning process.

The organisation's budget and financial targets are critical components of how culture is communicated through the organisation. Employees infer the relative importance of functions and their work for the coming year through an understanding of how the budgets and resources have been allocated for both 'business as usual'-related tasks and projects. Communicating the basis transparently is critical to building trust with employees.

The working environment needs to be supported by appropriate information of quality and timeliness that enables employees to discharge their decision-making effectively, within the accountability and authority delegated to them as outlined in their role profiles. This clarity of responsibilities in role profiles supports discussions with those employees who have pushed boundaries beyond their remit. All employees should know that if they breach policies, they will be subject to an appropriate level of disciplinary action, which applies equally to senior management as well as more junior employees.

This highlights the importance of the relationship between the CRO and the human resources (HR) director. Additionally, the HR director can assist with the development of risk and compliance training that goes beyond the feel of an electronic 'tick box' process to which management appears to give little attention and for which sanctions for non-completion are rarely enacted. The HR team can assist in developing a training programme for all levels that incorporates the understanding of risk as a threat and provider of opportunities. In support of the working environment;

1. Do you spend time helping staff to understand the measures they use operationally and how these support the delivery of the strategy?
2. Where tolerances have been articulated, do people understand why and what should happen if tolerances and limits are breached?
3. How much time do you spend with staff face to face when communicating and how much time is spent corresponding via email or by telephone?

Finally, CRO can work with the HR and audit teams to ensure redundant and low-value rules, policies and controls are removed to provide space so that employees can be guided by principles and encouraged to apply ethical judgment, building a sense of trust.

There is a drive across Europe to return to principles-based regulation rather than rules-based regulation. This approach puts the onus back on the companies to do the right thing rather than playing the margins of rules. This type of framework needs to be backed up with sanctions against those who do not behave in a way that supports the establishment of an adult relationship with the management. Without sanctions, the principles are meaningless.

Table 9.1 Signs of weakness and strength in culture

Signs of weakness	Risk culture factor	Signs of strength
Behaviours driven by ego and greed creating an environment in which employees fear speaking up.	Leaders as role models	Behaviours of humility, courage and self-control give rise to passion for the company's fate and fortunes.
There is an inconsistency between the brand and reputation that is communicated to external stakeholders, and the internal set of behaviours.		Positive view of brand and reputation of the organisation externally is consistent with its internal set of behaviours CEO visibly and actively challenges areas of high growth, profitability and return.
Management's verbal messages are inconsistent with their behaviours.		Risk management responsibilities reside with a CRO who reports to the CEO, is influential in decision-making, and is known to employees.
Unchallengeable relationships exist between members of the executive team, serving to create 'social silences'.		There is an open and honest ability to constructively challenge actions and preconceptions at all levels of the organisation.
Desires of a single directive leader dominate, preventing employees from challenging strategies, targets, behaviours and ideas for fear of the consequences.		Executives and managers demonstrate a consistent model of behaviours and standards, which are applied to all.
Constructive challenge has been replaced with fragmented information flows and engagement, shouting, and difficult personality issues.		Mistakes are actively acknowledged and lessons learned (tolerate and train staff for errors of judgment, do not tolerate errors of principle).
Management delegate too much accountability and do not take ownership or responsibility for the outcomes of actions of staff.		Business decisions are based on assessing possibility, profitability and principles.
Management and employees feel inhibited about passing on bad news or learning from past mistakes because errors of judgment are not accepted.		

	Recognition and reward	
The significant element of remuneration is performance related, where performance is measured on return generation, volume or market share with little value attributed to the assessment of risk and behaviours.		Recognition and respect exist for each other's talents, with differences celebrated.
Remuneration structure encourages a silo mentality and approach to risk management.		Business, risk and audit are all equally seen as adding value to the organisation.
Performance drivers of business units that show continuous 'outperformance' are not reviewed.		Remuneration evidences balance between growth objectives, risk management objectives, and behaviours.
Business unit performance objectives are not equally stretching.		Performance measures encourage people to do the right thing and think about the organisation as a whole rather than be a series of silos.
Reward and promotions are grounded in creating a 'first-across-the-line' competition among staff, discouraging cooperation and support for peers' discharging their responsibilities and accountabilities.		Business unit performance is regularly reviewed to ensure drivers of outperformance are understood.
The leadership does not communicate how strategy, risk appetite and operational performance measures align.		Business units' performance objectives are regularly reviewed for consistency in the level of stretch and challenge.
Risk information is sparse, slow and lacks insight to business implications.		Opportunities are taken to praise employees who exhibit good risk behaviours.
Risk information does not support developing discussions about risk and response plans.		The Board is fully engaged in setting the risk strategy, appetite, tolerances and operational limits that are consistent with the goals and resources of the company, the expectations of the Board and other stakeholders.
Risk reporting by exception provides a view of management disinterest.		The key performance measures are clear, identifiable, and linked from strategy through to the operational limits.
		The management of the evolution of the risk profile is a core component of the planning process.
		Risk information is timely and accurate, providing business insight that engages management in discharging their risk-related responsibilities.

Continued

Table 9.1 Continued

Signs of weakness	Risk culture factor	Signs of strength
		Decisions are assessed against complete risk-reward criteria. The Group and business units approaches to measuring and monitoring risk-taking and risk management are consistent. Cultural and behavioural alignment is assessed at the point of recruitment, and monitored and developed annually. There is tolerance and training of staff for errors of judgment, and errors of principle are not tolerated.
Governance structure, role profiles and responsibilities do not identify delegated authorities and responsibilities for managing and reporting risks. Risk management is viewed as a compliance exercise and thus a preserve of the risk function to manage. Risk function is not independent of the business and engaged as the final sign-off in decision-making. Functions performing activities relating to risk measurement and monitoring, and risk-taking and management are not separate such that the business has the ability to manipulate the reported risk positions. Business units behave in a tribal manner and look out for their own, feeling no responsibility for the performance or issues resulting from the wider Group.	Working environment	Governance structure is transparent with clearly defined roles and responsibilities, where all know the limits of delegated authority. The responsibilities for risk management at the interfaces between the business, risk and audit are clearly defined, cohesive and consistently discharged across the organisation. Senior managers' risk-related responsibilities, including delegated authorities to take action, are included within their role profiles and are known publicly. Risk management is an integral part of all business processes (for example, strategic planning, performance management, underwriting and claims management) such that it is not thought of as a separate activity or part of completing a proposal for approval. There is no conflict of interest between functions performing the activities relating to risk measurement and monitoring and those relating to risk-taking and management.

There are frequent breaches of procedures, limits are ignored and the quality of risk reporting is not deemed a priority.

Communications with various stakeholders about risks that the company faces are not consistent and transparent, causing confusion for employees discharging responsibilities.

Decisions are taken without consideration of the implications for both risk and return.

Few proposals or decisions have been rejected on the basis of failing to meet risk-related criteria or corporate ethics.

The organisation risk management capabilities are allowed to 'age' and become misaligned with modern techniques, market demands and risks as they evolve.

Risk policies are annually reviewed and updated with little impact on day-to-day management of the business as a result of lack of usability and relevance.

Lack of engagement and passion for the company's fate leads to an apathy such that risk limit breaches are not acted upon or viewed as necessary to report with a sense of urgency.

Risk strategy has been articulated in a way that enables the organisation to enter and exit threats and opportunities in a timely manner.

Reporting to both internal and external stakeholders is consistent, identifying the threats and opportunities to the company.

Decisions are taken in a framework that understands the implications for the optimisation of the risk-return trade-off, which provides an early view of risks and opportunities supporting proactive actions.

Evidence exists of proposals that have been rejected on the basis of failing to meet risk-related criteria or corporate ethics.

Risk management policies and procedures are used within the business with evidence of active monitoring of compliance.

Risk limit breaches are escalated immediately and subsequently resolved.

Action is taken to ensure risk limit breaches do not recur. Management can interpret risk information and apply judgment in decision-making based on understanding how risk has been assessed and limitations of the approaches.

Continued

Table 9.1 Continued

Signs of weakness	Risk culture factor	Signs of strength
Risk information is not actively updated to maintain a complete radar of risks to the business.		Management understand the gaps and shortcomings in their risk information, can apply judgment effectively while seeking to enhance their capabilities.
The gaps in risk information are not understood, and plans do not exist to enhance capability.		Management regularly benchmarks its risk management understanding, frameworks and capabilities as techniques, markets and risks evolve.
Managers lack an understanding of how risk is assessed and the limitations of these assessments, resulting in expert judgment being applied inappropriately in decision-making.		Risk capabilities are clearly defined and competencies regularly assessed for effectiveness with gaps closed between current and desired capabilities.
Managers' understanding of how to interpret risk information is limited, resulting in actions not being taken in a timely manner or with the desired outcome.		Staff training on risk management includes education on both upside and downside risks.
Staff training targets the delivering evidence of compliance with regulations.		Evaluate the risk culture through feedback from staff, perhaps by inclusion in an existing annual staff survey as well as information from exiting staff.
Rules and policies are not actively enforced.		Redundant and low-value rules, policies and controls have been eliminated.
		Sanctions applied to those that breach rules and policies.

9.6   Signals of weakness and strength in culture

Table 9.1 illustrates factors that indicate strengths and weaknesses in culture, providing a sense of the level of risk that the company's culture may present.

9.7   Monitoring the risk culture

Table 9.2 outlines questions that the Board should consider to gain an understanding of potential issues regarding its risk culture. We are not suggesting that these issues always exist within these circumstances, nor that any negative outcomes are based in conscious attempts by employees to manipulate perceptions, but they can be the result of genuine attempts to find a solution to deliver for the company, however, without full recognition of the consequences. Many of these questions relate to when times are good, as these are the most difficult times for employees to speak out and flag issues, especially if their views could be counterintuitive interpretations of signals.

Imagine the following question as an employee speaks to his or her manager:

'Business is going well and we are winning industry awards, so why are you being so negative about the way we have priced it?'

As culture is based on many non-quantitative aspects, it is not possible to develop a fully objective framework for assessing the pressures on culture as certain aspects will always rely on subject assessment. Thus, pressure points are likely to be best assessed using a 'flash' survey to assess whether the company is developing in such a way that the culture is being put under pressure and may need a closer review.

We find that culture is most challenged when the people making the decisions are forced to assess which values and ambitions are the most important to them. These occasions can arise when

1. an organisation is significantly divergent from its strategic ambition, and is relying on innovation, financial re-engineering or a significant amount of action to control the business;
2. an individual perceives that his or her prospects for career progression are materially deviating from their planned ambition, for example, as a result of competition for roles.

Table 9.2 Questioning potential risk culture hot spots

Key risk driver	Questions	Explanation
Balance sheet engineering	– How much financial engineering has been required to secure the balance sheet to support the new business growth requirements? – How frequently have we changed assumptions to 'squeeze out margins'?	– A business facing financial challenges may seek to take all opportunities to minimise the perceived risk that is being taken. With so much focus on the details of delivering results, it is possible that actions are undertaken that would otherwise be rejected and that a 'survival instinct' takes over as employees become naturally focussed on protecting themselves from the knock-on effects of potential adverse downside outcomes.
Growing new business and profitability	– Is new business growth significant relative to historic performance? Conversely, is the new business growth significantly below plan? – Is there a significant change in the market position / share? – Is there significant growth in new markets or areas with innovative new products? – How many key products are open to a significant volume of new business? – How often have we reviewed the pricing assumptions? Have the reviews weakened the pricing basis improving the price?	– Significant new business growth or the reliance on a single product can create an environment in which employees become reticent about being the 'bearer of bad news'. – In the lead-up to the credit crisis of 2008, the volume of mortgage applications resulted in staff accepting shortcuts in application requirements in order to manage the process. If a company experiences an escalation in its growth rate or volume of business it must manage, employees may take shortcuts in an attempt to ensure they continue to meet service standards. This may result in 'checks and balances' not being performed, or risks being underwritten in a way that is not anticipated in the pricing. With large volume growth, it is worth asking additional questions as evidence supporting how processes and infrastructure are coping with the demand. – Significant growth in markets resulting from innovative new products should be reviewed to ensure that it does not result from an error in pricing or assessment of the risks. – Where a company has effectively become reliant on a single product for its existence, managers may choose not to review the basis on which it has been priced for fear of it leading to closure, or they may keep it competitive with ever-increasing aggressive changes in the basis on which it is priced.

Targets and outperformance	– Is there an area that is making significant profits? – Is there a team that continually outperforms? – Were employees involved in challenging and setting the stretch performance targets? – Is there a reasonable work-life balance, or are key resources being stretched to deliver on 'must have' projects?	– There are numerous examples of banks at which traders have performed extremely well for the business, only for these results to be less-than-accurate reflections of the true position. The same could be said of teams that continuously outperform where the nature of their objectives may not be overtly stretching or management pressure employees to do what it takes to maintain market perceptions. – The Board needs to ensure that independent deep dives occur in order for it to understand what is driving the good performance. – Performance targets set by executives without input from their team can result in pressure on employees to deliver at all costs so as to ensure the executive receives his bonus and does not 'lose face' in front of the Board. Additionally, when executives have bid for and committed to projects, there is a risk that key personnel within the business are being over-stretched on too many 'must have' projects. This can result in shortcuts, work-arounds and sub-optimal implementations. This can be a sign that friction or competition between executives is surfacing as they compete for a limited resource pot to deliver for their 'silo'.
People movements	– How significant is the level of recruitment? – How significant is the number of leavers? – What is the turnover rate in assurance functions?	– New recruits need training to ensure that they reach the appropriate level of confidence to do the job that is required of them. This requires managers and staff to commit time to training, which can impact their resource stretch until the new recruits become operationally effective. During this time, the additional resource stretch could manifest itself in shortcuts in processes or new recruits being 'put to work' before they are ready, which could result in an increased number of complaints from customers or errors in what is being produced.

Continued

Table 9.2 Continued

Key risk driver	Questions	Explanation
		– Particular hot spots will be teams with significant staff shortages or vacancies to fill, which result in the most strain on current staff and greater pressure to get the new recruits to work.
		– The turnover rate in the assurance functions could be reflective of frictions between the business and the assurance teams as the assurance team tries to challenge what is being done within the business. A review of their reasons for leaving or of exit interview notes may reveal concerns that they were not confident enough to raise while in employment.
Rejected initiatives	– How many proposals and management actions have been rejected on the grounds of failing to meet the risk assessment criteria or of being outside the scope of the company's principles?	– If no proposals have failed to fall outside the bounds that the company would find acceptable, there is a risk that either the criteria for assessment, such as the risk appetite, are too broad, or that the assessments are being fitted within the criteria and are not necessarily reflective of the underlying exposure.
Systems and infrastructure	– Do we get the right data at the right time? – Does the information we receive rely on a significant number of manual approximations and adjustments being made? – Is a lot of the information we ask for being produced for the first time?	– The pressure to produce information that is appropriate and timely can mean that, with the best intentions, employees implement manual solutions that produce less-than-robust solutions and approximations. This means the data may not be as accurate as we believe for the decisions that we make. – This could be particularly the case if information is being presented for the first time, in which case it may be likely that systems have not been developed to cater for the specific output requirements. A key follow-up is to ensure that management have evidenced how plans allow for time to develop the production capabilities for the new information.

- How much spare capacity do we have so that we can cater for fluctuations in demand for information technology or information technology (IT) capacity?

- The management of spare capacity is critical to ensuring that fluctuations in demand for IT capacity can be managed. There is a company at which actuarial students had to go to the local PC store with a credit card to buy computing power to enable the year-end valuation to be completed. This was a result of a number of actuarial teams having simultaneous demands of computing resource that all had implications for the year-end results.

Personal ambition

- How do we know our executives are not promoting and embedding 'yes men'?
- When did we hear last from a manager who was openly challenging the ideas and direction of senior management proposals?
- When did we last hear bad news or of a significant risk event occurring?
- Are there signs of friction between teams?
- How do we know our team managers are actively cooperating with and supporting each other in the delivery of what is best for the company?
- Does management motivate by creating competition between staff members?

- The desire to maintain career progression can manifest itself as a lack of willingness to challenge executives who may influence employees' opportunities to progress, and the creation of a compensation structure in which the size of an individual's financial reward is partly dependent on what can be done to reduce the allocation to a 'competitor'.
- These behaviours can lead to a decline in the level of cooperation between businesses and prevent challenges and learning from mistakes.
- These hot spots may need to be addressed with executive coaching and a review of the approach to remuneration.
- When did we last sit down with members of executive's management teams in an informal way?

Continued

Table 9.2 Continued

Key risk driver	Questions	Explanation
	– Do performance reviews consist of ranking and comparing employees with each other and fixing a distribution? – Is the pot of money for bonuses fixed and to be shared among staff such that some must lose for others to gain? – Are those who are promoted those who are star performers for delivering performance and living the values? Are others fired or do they leave soon after a review?	

These divergences could be positive or negative, with a combination of these potentially leading to a high risk of cultural decline. This cultural decline may not be company-wide but localised to a specific team that is facing a challenge. For example, a large volume of new business growth may put pressure on managers within a customer services team to maintain service levels by foregoing quality assurance and sign-off procedures.

In the boom years of the mortgage market prior to the financial crisis of 2008, there was a marked decrease in the level of checking that companies undertook for mortgage applications. Brokers became significantly less fussy about checking the details of whether a customer could meet the mortgage repayments. The underpinning of such behaviour could have been to keep track with volumes of business or a complacency towards the risk being mitigated by the checking process. In the end, customers' inability to meet repayments when house prices were depressed was critical to the fortunes of many banks.

10
The Board and the New Chief Risk Officer

This chapter provides an understanding of the contributions the Board and the chief executive officer (CEO) make to assist the chief risk officer (CRO) build a vision for risk management that the business values. In particular, it illustrates

– the role of the Board in risk management,
– the contribution of the CEO to support the risk function,
– the role of the CRO, and
– a structure for developing a risk management vision.

10.1   Role of the Board in risk management

A Board of directors is a legal requirement, with the rationale being to ensure that the company is making decisions with regard to the interests of all its relevant stakeholders, and is not just driven by the interests of senior management or a dominant individual.

A company looks to develop and grow a business in a way that balances the expectations, risks and rewards of all stakeholders through taking opportunities for which the outcome will have a level of uncertainty in a marketplace that continuously evolves and changes. The Board's role is to ensure that it is in a position in which it can provide confidence and honest assurance to investors and other stakeholders that these uncertainties are understood and are being managed – that is, that the business has an effective risk management capability.

– Honest assurance is provided by being able to evidence that the approach to risk-taking balances the needs of all stakeholders, encouraging

growth and innovation without creating unacceptable exposures to risks.
– Confidence is established by evidencing that the Board makes decisions about risk-return optimisation strategies in full awareness of the implications for the Group as a whole, through its holistic view of the risks and the expected returns.

The Board's cornerstone in building this assurance and confidence is the recruitment of an appropriate CEO, who is fit and proper to manage a business in the interests of all its various stakeholders. Risk management is not just a process, but depends on people's behaviours, which are dictated by the culture that the CEO brings to the organisation. The CEO is likely to recruit individuals to his or her executive team who support a similar cultural approach, which will further embed a set of behavioural norms across the organisation. Similarly, the CEO's attitude to risk management is critical. Experience has shown that when the CEO is indifferent to risk management and treats it as a compliance exercise, the CRO is powerless, risk culture is non-existent, and the Board is ill-informed and ill-prepared for managing the vagaries of the business.

In order to understand the behaviours and skills that are required of the new CEO, it is important that the Board understands the boundaries of behaviour that it believes to be 'off limits' and unacceptable. These then form the basis of the cultural assessment of the candidates. These boundaries and limits must be supported by the CEO and embedded within the organisation over his or her years in office. The Board must ensure that the message is reinforced through actions being taken against those who breach these boundaries of behaviour and activity.

The appointment of the CEO usually includes a coming together of minds on a general strategic direction for the business for which a process is undertaken to articulate the plan.

As an outturn of the strategic planning process, the Board should ensure that it has a plan that details a set of objectives and outlines how it will deliver on these objectives over the plan horizon. This plan should show an understanding of the risks that it brings to the business, the impact in the event that these risks materialise, and how they can be managed or mitigated. Once the Board has agreed upon a plan, there needs to be a clear understanding of how this cascades into the way in which it will be delivered over the coming year, including how the delivery will be overseen, and how decisions will be made and risks monitored and managed.

This requires an understanding of

1. how the strategic plan is developed and its delivery monitored over the coming year;
2. how performance is measured and rewarded;
3. how products and services are developed and priced;
4. how capital and solvency are managed;
5. how risks are identified, assessed, monitored and managed; and
6. how the governance framework (and information) operates across the company to ensure all decisions are made by the right individuals in a timely manner and aligned to delivering the objectives.

Under the European Solvency 2 regime, this may be an articulation of the demands of the Own Risk and Solvency Assessment (ORSA).

10.2   Role of the chief executive in risk management

As enterprise risk management (ERM) is integral to the running and management of the business, the CEO is acknowledged to be the ultimate CRO, responsible for ensuring that ERM is embedded and used within the business. This is why the CEO's engagement is vital to risk management, as it is not only about the reporting and the infrastructure of the business, but the way in which people behave. Employees will look to the executive team for role models and will only feel comfortable to 'speak up' and openly challenge if the CEO is visibly willing to ask questions about risk at times when things look as if they are going extremely well.

Historically, the recruitment of CEOs followed interesting patterns. Generally, in benign markets, CEOs were appointed who had a strong competence in growing the distribution capability of the business. When financial markets became volatile, the CEO's core competencies switched to that of managing expense control effectively, getting better returns at lower costs. Going forward, the demands are going to grow on the CEO's risk management competencies.

The CEO will look to the CRO to bring strategic insight from the risk information., for example, the CEO will want to know

1. which exposures could force him or her to change the strategic agenda to damage limitation, such as
   a. what could cause the risk to materialise and how quickly it could manifest itself;

    b. what options he or she has to prevent it from happening now;

    c. what he or she can do to reduce the size of the impact;

    d. how much it will cost to take these actions;

    e. which employees have their eyes on the ball and the authority to act should things start to happen.

2. what risk and return the new initiative brings to the table, such as

    a. how it impacts his or her overall risk-return profile;

    b. whether there are new risks and what the capability is to manage them;

    c. whether the risks are the source of return;

    d. why you think you have the capability to manage them better than your peers;

    e. who is signed up to deliver the benefit and who is managing the risks.

10.3 The chief risk officer (CRO)

10.3.1 The role of the chief risk officer

The role of the CRO has evolved over a number of years. There is plenty of literature that charts the develop of risk functions over the last decade from one that monitors controls and loss events, through downside risk mitigation support, to the latest view of supporting the understanding and exploitation of risk to achieve greater return. The latest evolution requires the skill set of the CRO to evolve further into one that can assess and provide insight on the strategic direction of the business and the implications for the risk-return trade-off.

Many CROs now report directly to the CEO, which has brought increased prominence to risk functions. With increased prominence comes the need to ensure the organisation understands and values the contribution the function makes to the business. As such, the business needs to understand clearly the position the risk function is taking on issues, which the CRO can achieve through an 'endorse or escalate' approach. As the business engages the risk function through the development of a proposition, it is seeking an explicit position, either a positive endorsement of the proposal, or a decision that certain aspects of the proposal are such that it feels the need to escalate its concerns for a final decision to a higher forum. Initially, the escalation may go to an executive risk committee prior to reporting to the Board risk committee. This provides a 'no surprises' approach for the executive team and an opportunity to prepare for a more informed and constructive debate in the risk committee.

To provide this clarity for the business, a number of risk functions base this explicit assessment (to endorse or escalate) against a set of criteria as to whether the proposal

i.   aligns with the company's strategic direction, risk strategy, appetite and policies;
ii. is legally possible, profitable and aligns with the company's principles[1];
iii. provides an appropriate consideration to both threats and opportunities, risk and return, including whether new risks and opportunities have been created;
iv. provides an appropriate assessment of the key risk sensitivities[2] and how these will be monitored to ensure the business delivers on the proposal or knows when alternative actions are needed;
v.   identifies management actions and response plans that are reasonable and appropriate[3], with responsibilities and triggers that are clear and well understood.

The Board will expect a CRO on the executive team to be the individual who will act as their conscience on a daily basis, someone who is able to ask the questions of their executive colleagues that the Board should and would be asking if they were working within the business on a day-to-day basis[4].

The CRO needs to be able to convert the data from the models into a real-world context with real-world examples, providing insight to risk positions wider than just at the positions required by regulation, but at more and less extreme positions in a way that enables the Board to use their many years of experience to interpret the implications of, and determine the level of comfort they have with, the impacts such events would have on the business today and how management proposes to respond to them.

10.3.2   Vision for risk management

Taking up a position as a new CRO brings with it many challenges. Some of the early discussions will be with peers on the executive team, members of the non-executive community and external stakeholders seeking to find out about strengths and immediate key concerns. The next task may be to form a vision of how risk is integrated into the way the business is managed. Arguably, because culture is so closely linked with 'how things get done', the vision will naturally support the development of the right risk culture, as outlined in Table 9.2.

Table 10.1 provides some structure and initial scope from which to develop the risk management vision.

10.3.3   Skill set of a CRO

As the role of the CRO gains greater prominence and demands to be more strategic, the CRO requires a broad understanding of all key areas of the business and needs to be able to think as a strategist, understanding that the organisation must take risks to compete in the marketplace. In a small executive team that is enthused by opportunity or emotionally heightened in the midst of managing threats, the CRO needs to remain balanced, able to detach from situations, and step back and consider a view unclouded by his or her own feelings and the emotions of others. This can create frictions, as different individuals because of the nature of their positions, will accuse the CRO equally of being too risk averse and too aggressive over the same issue. This will require that the CRO be willing and able to think differently, take counterintuitive positions when the business appears to be booming, and be able to express a view directly, clearly and concisely while under attack from all sides.

As a member of the executive team, the CRO needs to be able to manage the conflict that comes with being part of an executive team, but not be viewed by employees as 'in bed with the management', such that they cannot approach the CRO with issues and concerns. The CRO needs to support the fostering of an open environment where in which constructive challenge is welcomed such that those with a passion for the organisation and its future can feel engaged in making sure it is guided appropriately with the interests of its various stakeholders in the mind.

Table 10.1   Initial scope for the risk management vision

	Vision
Executive risk Leadership	– Executives have humility, courage, self-control and passion.
	– The positive external brand image and reputation are consistent with the behaviours of management.
	– Executives table ideas with an expectation of being challenged and, potentially, ideas being rejected on risk-related or ethical grounds.
	– Executives expect their views to be questioned by peers and subordinates.
	– The CEO is actively seen to make decisions balancing both risk and return.
	– The CEO challenges areas in which equally good and bad performance occurs to ensure that, either it is genuine outperformance or action is being taken to correct the underperformance.
	– The CRO brings business insight to the executive team during strategic discussions.
	– The CRO is engaged early in processes and on decisions.
	– Executives respect what each individual brings to strategic business decisions, with functions working collaboratively in support of discharging all duties in the best interests of the organisation.
	– The CRO is known to staff members within the business who interact with customers, suppliers and other external stakeholders on a daily basis.
Governance framework	– The governance structure is simple, clear and transparent.
	– The authority that has been delegated is clearly articulated and allocated to the extent that each manager knows the bounds of what he or she can do, what he or she cannot do, and how he or she must go about getting decisions outside of his or her authority.
	– All risk-related responsibilities and authorities are regularly reviewed and updated within role profiles and committee terms of reference.
	– Risk responsibilities and interfaces within the organisation are clear and well understood.
	– Documentation of the governance structure, roles and responsibilities, and processes is clear, concise and used within the business on a day-to-day basis.
	– Reviews take place of any risk limit breaches to ensure they do not recur.
	– Action is taken to ensure any breaches of rules and policies are dealt with appropriately.
	– Activities that support risk measurement and monitoring are separate from risk management.
	– The risk management framework is regularly benchmarked against industry-planned future enhancements to practices, with plans developed to close any gaps identified.

Recognition, capabilities and training	– Performance incentives include risk-adjusted measures.
	– Performance incentives include non-financial risk-related measures such as risk limit, compliance and governance breaches.
	– Performance is measured over an extended period and adjusted for any underperformance.
	– The company rewards staff who deliver while 'living the values', using them as examples and role models from within the business to illustrate what is expected.
	– Proposed performance arrangement are backtested for reasonableness.
	– The remuneration committee seeks feedback from the CRO on proposed performance awards and structures.
	– Executives understand and can interpret risk information.
	– Executives understand the shortcomings of the information and the models used, and know how to apply judgments accordingly.
	– Organisation-wide risk capabilities are regularly benchmarked against evolving practice as the environment changes, and used to enhance understanding, information and the management of risk so that decision-making is improved.
	– The required risk capabilities are clearly defined and competencies regularly assessed for effectiveness, with gaps closed between current and desired capabilities.
	– Risk training is provided for all levels in the organisation and balances the understanding of both risk and opportunities.
	– Recruitment and initiation of staff include briefings and analysis of the company values and required behaviours.
Risk based decision making	– Risk is an integral part of standard business processes, performance management and decision-making.
	– Risk information flows freely, frequently and in a timely manner to support and evidence the management of the business within the delegated authorities.
	– Risk information is not subject to material manual adjustment or intervention.
	– Risk information is integrated with key business information used to make decisions and is not seen as a distinctly separate set of 'thermometers'.
	– The CRO hears bad news early, and what action is being taken to rectify the position and what is being done to prevent it happening again
	– Decisions have been rejected on risk-related and ethical grounds.
	– Decisions are made by understanding the impact on risk-adjusted performance, and they support the efficient allocation of capital.
	– Decisions are made using complete risk-reward criteria that include an assessment of the impact on the wider Group.
	– The risk register supports and enhances the operational delivery of key processes.
	– Risk strategy has been articulated in a way that enables the organisation to enter and exit adverse exposures in a timely manner.

Continued

Table 10.1 Continued

	Vision
	- Cost-benefit analysis is undertaken to assess the value of improvements to controls.
	- Redundant or low-value rules and controls are removed.
	- Risk information provides insight to the impact of decisions on the risk-return profile over the plan horizon.
	- Stress tests and scenarios provide useful insight, interpreting the mathematics into real-world events and vice versa.
	- Risk information is not reliant on a single methodology or statistic.
	- Early warning indicators have been developed from an understanding of the risk drivers that give rise to the adverse outcome.
	- Information regarding the control of risks includes the following clarity on actions – 'What? Why? When? Who? How?'
Risk strategy, appetite & tolerances	- Risk strategy informs the business strategy.
	- Risk appetite manages the volatility of key performance objectives.
	- Risk limits and tolerances support the operational process that occur day to day and help staff see how what they do helps deliver the strategy.
	- The CRO sees decisions and actions that actively need to be taken to manage within the boundaries that have been established.
Risk environment	- The company tolerates and trains staff for errors of judgment and aims to learn lessons to prevent these recurring, but does not tolerate errors of principle.
	- The business operates continuous improvement cycles.
	- Board instructions are translated into operational instructions, and the purpose is understood by those who interact with external stakeholders.
	- Questioning and challenging are seen as part of the process of getting approvals.
	- Risk management activities are undertaken because staff understand how they assist in delivering the strategy.

Appendices

Appendix A: Three Lines of Defence Operating Model

The three lines of defence model is emerging as the most common organisational structure that provides independence for risk and audit functions. This framework underpins the thinking in this book. Simply stated, the classical three lines of defence model has the following responsibility divisions:

Line 1 responsibilities

Line 1 is responsible for the day-to-day operation of the business. This responsibility means that it must implement and operate within the risk management and governance framework agreed upon by the Board on advice from the risk function.

Line 2 responsibilities

Effectively, line 2 is about providing a framework within which authority can be delegated from the Board to the frontline staff to enable them efficiently and effectively to deliver the strategy on a day-to-day basis within the boundaries and limits that have been established.

During the year, the risk function is charged with oversight and challenged to ensure the business is delivering the plan within the parameters that have been set, and that any significant deviations, arising from internal or external events, are identified early, with solutions 'endorsed or escalated' as appropriate.

Line 3 responsibilities

Audit is about providing assurance that the people, processes and controls within the organisation are operating effectively and as have been represented to the Board.

Appendix B: Framework for Developing Risk Strategy Statements

Table B.1 Examples of questions to support the development of risk strategy statements

Questions	Examples of potential resulting risk strategy statements
Will the business units operate independently on a day-to-day basis, but with alignment to Group practices and with Group oversight?	We have Group-wide risk governance and risk categorisation. We operate a Group-wide planning process and take an aggregated view of the organisation.
Will the Group steer business units to optimise returns based on Group diversified capital requirements or with each entity on a stand-alone basis?	Group diversification benefits are allocated to the business units to the extent they are realisable in practice.
Will the main metrics used internally be risk-adjusted value creation measures or some other measure?	Decisions are driven by risk-adjusted performance metrics designed to measure value creation from a shareholder perspective over the medium term. We do not wish to take unrewarded risks.
Will other metrics (e.g. profit) still flow into decision-making?	We will take on risks dependent on the expected return exceeding the cost of capital. We will take on risks that enhance the value of our diversification benefit to optimise the risk-return profile.
From whose perspective do you aim to focus on growing value?	We will charge a price for accepting risk that seeks to optimise our risk/reward profile and that fully reflects the cost of taking that risk. We will pass risk to a third party if the price is value enhancing.
Do you plan to act as an intermediary or use your own balance sheet to take risk?	We do not act as a risk intermediary, but aim to utilise our balance sheet to make returns on the capital employed. We do not want to take risks that are not consistent with the delivery of our strategy as an insurer.
What activities will form part of your strategy for value creation?	We take on other risks (such as persistency, expense, operational, etc.) as a consequence of selling our core products. We manage these risks to optimise the risk-adjusted return and where we have the people, skills and systems to manage them

What sort of risks do you want to take – which taken voluntarily and which are inherent in our business model – and is it important to be able to understand and manage the risks? Which parts of the value chain / production chain are you going to do in-house or to outsource? Where is the value-adding activity? What methods of distribution are important? Is your own brand one method of distribution?	We will take on insurance/underwriting risks where this is value additive. We will take on risks that we have the capability to understand and manage and which support the Group's aim of [...]. We will not take on excessive market risk except where it is a consequence of our core strategic objectives (e.g. where a revenue stream is exposed to market risk) We will not take on excessive credit risk from the financial market. We will accept exposure to counterparty failure within limits where this is a result of managing the risk exposures of the organisation. We will seek to exploit the less immediate cash flow demands from the contracts we have written to leverage an enhanced return from assets that reward those that can carry the illiquidity risk. We will manufacture products and administer business while the costs and benefits of doing this in-house are better than those achievable from outsourcing the arrangement (i.e. expense risk)
To what extent are you open to taking on concentration in terms of – products – risk types – sectors and names (e.g. counterparties) – business units?	We have clear strategies for taking risk and limits by risk type. We want to ensure our return is not reliant on a single revenue stream or risk type. We employ sector and name-level concentration limits. Operational risks are a consequence of doing business, but we do not want to expose ourselves to significant reputational damage or regulatory censure, which is out of line with our appetite. We incentivise diversification. We manage diversification through balancing the exposure to our business units, which results in a target mix of X% life business and Y% general insurance business.
What are the constraints imposed by the customer group?	Our risk-taking activities and decisions should not cause undue customer detriment, in favour of shareholders. We will aim to keep policy lapses at low levels which result from customer dissatisfaction. We will aim to design our products to meet customer needs.

Appendix C: Pragmatic Approach to Filtering Stress and Scenarios

Table C.1 provides an example of a quick and simple way of filtering ideas generated from SST workshops to ensure that the process that it is supporting does not grind to a halt.

Table C.1 illustrates how scenarios can be assessed for their implications on all the dimensions of the risk appetite framework. This can help with widening the thought process to be more than focused on a financial loss figure. The determination of the impact as high (H), medium (M), or low (L) is made on a subject basis. Having populated the grid, it is possible to determine which of the scenarios are worth more detailed investigation.

Table C.1   High-level filtering of scenarios

Category	Stress and scenarios	Mitigating actions	Risk Appetite: Prob	Impact - Financial Elements Capital	Earnings	Liquidity	Impact - Franchise Elements Customers & distributors	Regulators & legislators	Capital markets	Operational delivery
Single factors			..%	H	M	L	M	M	M	M
			..%	H	L	L	M	M	M	L
			..%	M	L	L	H	L	M	L
Key assumptions			..%	L	H	L	L	L	M	L
			..%	M	H	L	L	H	M	L
			..%	M	M	L	L	L	M	L
Market outlook/ synthetic scenarios			..%	L	H	L	L	L	M	L
			..%	H	H	M	M	M	H	L
			..%	M	M	L	L	L	M	L
Historic experience			..%	M	M	L	M	H	M	L
			..%	M	M	L	L	M	L	L
			..%	L	L	L	L	L	L	L
Company experience			..%	L	M	L	H	H	L	L
			..%	L	M	L	M	M	H	L
			..%	M	M	M	H	H	M	L

Appendix D: Supporting Challenge in the ALM Committee

Table D.1 outlines some questions that can support understanding the appropriateness of investment opportunities. It is appropriate to recognise the paper 'Understanding the Risks in New Asset Classes' by Christopher Chappell et al. (2007), which documented thinking in this space.

Table D.1 Generic questions to challenge investment opportunities

Consideration	Questions for consideration	Comments and sign-offs	Document reference

Description of the investment opportunity	1. Explain how the investment works
	   a. Is the return based on capital appreciation or an income stream?
	   b. How are payments made and the final settlement repaid?
	 2. What are the cash flows that occur?
	   a. Describe the components of any cash flows (e.g. coupons, payment in kind, etc.).
	   b. What proportion of the income comes from each source?
	 3. When do these cash flows occur?
	 4. What will give rise to a change in the cash flows?
	   a. What is the underlying driver of profits from which these cash flows will be paid?
	 5. Outline any guarantees or preferential entitlements.
	 6. Confirm whether this is a direct investment in an asset or an investment through a third party
	   a. Explain the nature of any underlying asset and evidence that it exists.		

Return expectation	1. What is the return expectation?
	   a. Are there comparable investments the history of which we can examine or against which we can benchmark the proposed return for reasonableness?
	 2. What gives rise to the return?
	   a. Is the investment/return geared?
	   b. Does the investment arbitrage regulatory regimes or tax regimes in order to enhance returns?		

Continued

Table D.1 Continued

Consideration	Questions for consideration	Comments and sign-offs	Document reference
	c. Does the investment rely on benign regulatory or other regimes in order to make returns?		
	d. Does the investment have an underlying track record (i.e. is there a proven profit stream already or is this an investment in a new project that is projecting to see profits in the future (e.g. some infrastructure investments)?		
	e. Is the profit stream reliant on the quality of the management team in place, and what is their track record on delivery? What is the likelihood of their moving on? What may drive them to consider this and what would be the impact?		
	f. Is the investment (or profit streams) dependent on social trends, consumer behaviour or changes to market demands (e.g. renewable energy sources) that could introduce risk to return achievability?		
	g. Is there a theoretical 'free lunch'/pricing anomaly?		
	3. What are the risks to the profits not being made?		
	4. Who is backing any guarantees?		
	5. What would make this investment unattractive (What would squeeze the margin? competition? targeting of company finance structures, e.g. increased debt multiples?)?		
	6. What would give rise to the returns not being achieved?		
	7. If the investment is a commitment of funds over the next few years, explain what might happen that could mean the expected return could be squeezed.		
Assessment of whether the return results from a selective marketing push	1. Is this a fashionable push on diversification or return under which historic returns look good because of the timing of money flows into or out of the investment, gearing or point in cycle (e.g. technology and housing bubbles)?		
	2. Can we explain all aspects of the data (return, volatility, correlations) in terms of what we know about the way the product has been put together?		

Return expectations being foregone	3. What is being sold to fund the investment, and thus what is the adjusted enhancement?
	4. What opportunities/market timing might we be foregoing by entering the commitment?
Expenses	5. What charges and expenses may arise?
	6. How does the remuneration and fee structure operate?
	a. Do these charges and expenses change based on performance or some other measure?
	b. Are the fees fixed or how could they change? Are we liable for any expense 'overrun'?
	c. How do the fees impact the return in various circumstances? If things go very well, is the performance dampened? If things go poorly, what happens?
	d. How does the remuneration incentivise good investment management/oversight?
	7. How are all parties in this transaction being remunerated?
	a. What are the areas for potential conflicts of interest?
	b. What is the nature of any relationship between parties recommending the investment, managing any fund and running the actual investment?
	c. Outline any revenue/compensation (financial or otherwise) that flows between these parties and for what purposes.
	8. What happens if the investment is exited early?
	9. Will the remuneration to other parties and the cost of any additional internal resource or system requirement impact the investment expense assumption? How much?
	10. How will these be treated in the accounts? What is the impact on the discount rate used for the liabilities?
	11. How is the performance fee structure being modelled in the actuarial models?

Continued

Table D.1 Continued

Consideration	Questions for consideration	Comments and sign-offs	Document reference
Taxation	1. How is the investment treated for tax purposes?		
	2. What are the risks of challenge from tax authorities?		
	3. Does a taxation history exist?		
	4. Is the proposed tax treatment likely to change as a result of its introduction (e.g. assets based on arbitrage)?		
Legal/Corporate structure	1. What is the structure of the investment?		
	a. How complex is the investment structure (evidence this)? Identify that the actual underlying asset exists.		
	b. Is the structure transparent?		
	c. Could the structure be used for money laundering?		
	2. What entities are involved in this structure and what are their roles?		
	a. Which legal entity issues this investment?		
	b. Under which legal jurisdiction is the instrument constructed?		
	c. Is the product dependent on the solvency of any other entity?		
	3. What are the geographical locations of these entities?		
	a. What is the political stability of the countries involved?		
	b. Does the country have a stable regulatory framework that is up to international standard?		
	c. How easy is it going to be to get money out of a country should the investment/markets deteriorate?		
	d. Do the geographical locations breach any corporate social or ethical responsibility standards?		
	4. What are the reasons for choosing this structure and these geographical locations?		
	5. Who are the controlling interests in these entities?		
	a. Is there scope for conflict of interest?		

Details of the parties involved in the opportunity	1. Who are the fund managers?
	2. What is their track record with this type of investment?
	3. Do the fund managers/advisers meet corporate criteria for use, or could they give rise to damage to reputation or people risk?
	4. Are the fund managers reputable and will they want to ensure investments do not perform badly because of their reputation and need to seek investors for future opportunities?
	5. Is there any potential bias in advice being provided?
	6. Does the seller have more expertise than we do in relation to this investment?
	a. How much do we trust the seller?
	b. How have we tried to get independent verification and ensure there is no conflict of interest?
	7. Does the third party appear to understand the risks it is taking?
	a. Is it open about these risks?
	b. Is the third party open about how it will manage/mitigate these risks?
Currency	1. Are we invested outside of our local jurisdiction and in what currencies?
	2. What are the currency risks and are they hedged back?
	3. Will there be basis risk?
	4. Are there local currency matching requirements?
Diversification	1. What diversification benefit does this investment provide?
	2. Do we understand why this diversification benefit exists?
	3. What is the information on which this assertion has been based?
	4. Is there historic experience of the underlying, or similar assets that has been used to determine these assumptions? What expert judgement has been applied?
	5. How do our other correlation assumptions change?
	a. Does the investment contain risks that are correlated to others in our portfolio?
	6. How does this impact the overall risk-return optimisation?

Continued

Table D.1 Continued

Consideration	Questions for consideration	Comments and sign-offs	Document reference
Execution and settlement	1. What is the process for executing the transaction? 2. How will the execution be managed to avoid moving market prices? 3. Is there opportunity for a third party to become involved in the misappropriation of funds? 4. How do funds get from our accounts to a third party? 5. Who is the administrator?		

Collateralisation	1. Describe any underlying asset backing the investment that could be used as security.
	2. Are we/others required to post collateral?
	3. With what frequency is the collateral amount re-assessed?
	4. With whom is the collateral posted and how is it 'ring-fenced'?
	5. What is the form of any collateral that can be posted?
	  a. What are the risks associated with that type of collateral?
	  b. Can we value them easily?
	  c. What are the skills and ability to manage the assets should we receive them?
	  d. Would we be able to sell it on? How does the term of this collateral compare to the assets being 'covered'?
	6. In adverse circumstances, will the marking of collateral increase?
	7. Do we have our own independent model and data feeds from which to assess the collateralisation?
	  a. At what level does a difference in view on the amount of collateral become material?
	  b. What is the process for resolving any differences of opinion on the amount of collateral required?
	8. Consider the security of any counterparty who has hold of our assets.
	9. Are there implications for our earnings volatility or liquidity requirements?		

Governance and control of the investment	1. How are the investments controlled/governed?
	  a. Explain the roles and responsibilities.
	  b. Are there other investors and how is this structured?
	2. Do we have control of the investment decisions, or are we transferring these to a third party (e.g. fund manager)?
	  a. What control do we have or is it just an advisory capacity?
	  b. If it is advisory, what are the options if we do not like the manager, or the investments perform badly?
	3. Is there another party who will bear losses ahead of us?
	  a. What is their interest?
	  b. Is the investment a significant part of their portfolio? Will this make them actively interested in monitoring and preventing losses/burn through of their investment?
	  c. If we are invested through a fund manager, what is the nature of the relationship between the manager and these third parties?
	4. Who audits the fund manager's accounts and when?
	5. Do we have the opportunity to audit the fund manager's processes?
	6. Do we have the right to audit the fund manager's accounts and valuations?
	7. Is the investment regularly reviewed and monitored to prevent adverse events happening between reviews?
	8. How does the fund manager monitor the investment?
	  a. What does the fund manger's management information include (e.g. turnover and debt coverage ratios)?
	  b. How frequently does the fund manager receive it?

Implications for capital	1. What is the impact on the solvency position now and in the future? 2. Does the investment arbitrage our regulatory capital regime (what are the capital implications at confidence levels different from those required by the regulator)? 3. Does the investment increase our credit risk exposure to an existing counterparty?

Continued

Table D.1 Continued

Consideration	Questions for consideration	Comments and sign-offs	Document reference
Implications for liquidity	1. What are our contractual commitments?		
	2. Is the amount to be invested immediate, or will it be drawn down over a number of years? If it is to be drawn down, what will be done with the assets in the meanwhile?		
	3. Could our commitments extend beyond the term of the initial proposed investment (e.g. the assets may have a term of five years, but the commitment is to make funds available over the next five years, meaning the commitment is ten years)?		
	a. If so, is there any experience as to how much longer it could be before we could exit our investment?		
	4. With any non-cash settlements, will they be rolled over, and if so, in what form of asset/investment?		
	a. If payments can be retained and deferred, explain what might happen to these in adverse circumstances?		
	5. Can the loan (etc.) be repaid early or extended? Explain the consequences.		
	6. What is the size of the market?		
	7. How has it been developing in the past and is likely to develop in the future?		
	8. Is the structure of the investment easy to replicate so the market can develop?		
	9. Who has been investing to date?		
	10. Is there a secondary market for the investment?		
	a. How liquid is that secondary market?		
	b. Will it trade the asset, but only at a deep discount?		
	11. What is the prospect for future issuance, or supply-demand balance changes leading to changes in the liquidity profile?		
	12. Does the illiquidity of the investment have implications for the way in which the asset is accounted for?		
	a. If so, what is the risk that this could change?		

13. How can we unwind our position?

    a. What third parties, transaction costs, penalties and time frame would be involved?

14. If there is a requirement to roll our investment (e.g. options) close to expiry, will we be at a competitive disadvantage (e.g. a bank can charge more than a fair price to roll a complex structure)?

Implications for reputation	1. Is the investment exposed to any underlying that would not meet our social responsibility or ethical investment requirements (avoiding reputational damage)?
	2. Does the investment require actions that could harm our brand (e.g. aggressive debt collection, asset stripping)?
	3. Does the investment fit with expectations we have given customers?
	a. Is the investment to be used to back participating business or funds for which guidance exists on expectations of the policyholder?
	4. Does the investment comply with regulations (e.g. limitations on use of certain investment for the purposes of speculation)?
	5. Has the investment been reviewed by the regulator and tax authorities?
Implications for pricing and existing business	1. How would the investment alter our pricing bases?
	2. How would the investment impact our projections and illustration bases?
	3. How could this impact our new business volumes or persistency experience?
Implications for risk management	1. What is the impact of the investment on our risk appetite and tolerances?
	a. Do we understand the principle risks and threats inherent in this investment?
	b. How have the risks been identified and assessed?
	c. Are we reliant on the fund manager, advisers or other parties for this information?

Continued

Table D.1 Continued

Consideration	Questions for consideration	Comments and sign-offs	Document reference
	2. What is the impact on the internal model?		
	a. Does this require a model change, and if so, of what type?		
	b. Is it a major change and does it require regulatory pre-approval?		
	3. Who will be responsible for monitoring and reporting?		
	a. What is the process and what are the escalation triggers?		
	b. What does the management information look like (including key measures)?		
	4. What are the ongoing reporting requirements from the third party to us (e.g. frequency of reporting, ability for ad-hoc updates, frequency of writedown assessments, change in approach when the asset in under stress)?		
	5. What is the additional internal cost/time required for this?		
	6. What are the training needs?		
	7. Do we have any key personnel?		
Models	1. Details of how the investment will be modelled		
	2. Do we understand the principles on which the pricing model is based?		
	3. Is the model widely used in the industry and well understood?		
	4. What are the areas of approximation, simplification and expert judgment?		
Parameter estimation	1. Can we replicate the pricing model reasonably and independently?		
	a. What are the areas of approximation?		
	b. What are the key assumptions/simplifications?		
	c. What would make these inappropriate?		

2. How much data is available that is directly related to the type of investment?
3. How much data is available from perceived indirectly relevant data sources or comparable investments?
   a. What key assumptions/judgements have been made?
4. What are the sources from which we can validate the data?
   a. Are they independent?
5. How many market makers contribute to the historic performance data?
6. What sort of events could impact the value of the investment that may be missing from the historic data because of its sparsness?
7. How are we going to monitor its evolution?
8. If we are going to use regulatory standard approaches, these are broad brush. Does this investment arbitrage the risk assessment underpinning the standard formula parameter?
9. Do we have a sense of how the investment should perform in certain circumstances?
10. What would lead to margin squeezes, changes in any illiquidity premium, drivers of defaults, etc.?

Systems

1. Do we have systems to support the data management or will significant investment be required?
2. What other process will be impacted? Consideration should be given to:
   a. investment systems and processes
   b. accounting systems and processes
   c. actuarial models
   d. risk reporting
   e. solvency monitoring
3. Have the data requirements been specified to meet regulatory and legislative requirements?
4. Are there processes to change this, should demands change?
5. What is the cost?

Continued

Table D.1 Continued

Consideration	Questions for consideration	Comments and sign-offs	Document reference

Financial reporting	1. What are the currenting account positions of the investment:
	  a. Admissibility
	  b. Tax
	2. Outline any known future regulatory or legislative changes and the potential change in the accounting or tax position:
	3. Outline the approach to valuing the liabilities
	  a. Discount rate
	  b. Adjustment for fund manager performance fees
	  c. Illiquidity premium
	4. How frequently are asset valuations undertaken?
	5. How frequently are impairment adjustments made?
	6. What is the view of the external auditors?		

Appendix E: Example of a Risk Register Report Template

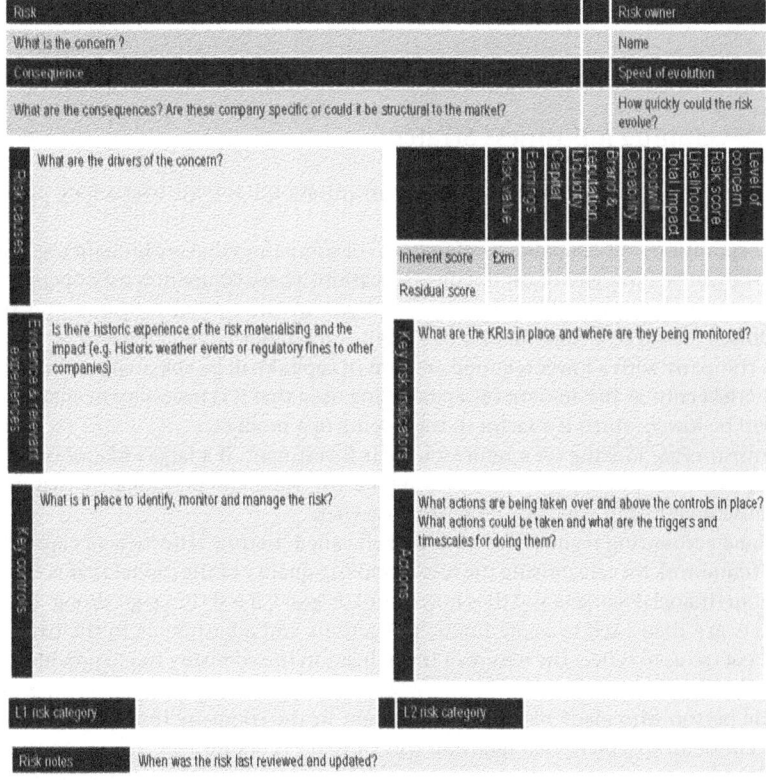

Risk		Risk owner
What is the concern ?		Name
Consequence		Speed of evolution
What are the consequences? Are these company specific or could it be structural to the market?		How quickly could the risk evolve?

Risk causes — What are the drivers of the concern?

Risk value · Earnings · Capital · Liquidity · Brand & reputation · Capacity · Goodwill · Total Impact · Likelihood · Risk score · Level of concern

Inherent score £xm

Residual score

Evidence & relevant experiences — Is there historic experience of the risk materialising and the impact (e.g. Historic weather events or regulatory fines to other companies)

Key risk indicators — What are the KRIs in place and where are they being monitored?

Key controls — What is in place to identify, monitor and manage the risk?

Actions — What actions are being taken over and above the controls in place? What actions could be taken and what are the triggers and timescales for doing them?

L1 risk category   L2 risk category

Risk notes   When was the risk last reviewed and updated?

Notes

3 Developing a Business Strategy

1. This may not be the same as what the organisation has done over a long period historically.
2. Corporations or Groups are combinations of companies that are brought together to optimise synergies or capital diversification. These companies may operate in the same sector or different ones (e.g., bank in the United Kingdom and the United States, or a combination of a bank, a retail outlet and an insurer).
3. A company with a lower required amount of capital will be able to price products more keenly, as the amount of capital being used that it is necessary to charge for will be lower, which is a factor in the pricing of a product.
4. Investors are looking for a return on their investment. If a large amount of their capital is not being put to work, this will cause a drag on performance that may cause investors to seek a better return elsewhere.
5. Some accounting regimes use an approach called 'tiering'. The 'tiers of capital' is a framework for categorising the loss-absorbing quality of the capital that is raised from financial markets and thus how useful or 'good' it is if things go wrong. These tiers are then used to apply limits, restrictions and adjustments to the balance sheets so as to reflect the nature of the obligation the company has to providers of each form of financing. Tier 1 is viewed as the 'best' at absorbing losses – that is, the person who made his or her investment in the company through an instrument or arrangement that falls into this category is taking a greater risk of losing all of his or her money than someone who uses an instrument classified in the next tier down. Types of capital that are good at absorbing losses are more useful from a company's perspective, as they increase financial flexibility, because more can be used in assessing the company's financial strength, but the capital is provided at a premium cost.
6. As with all providers of capital, their demands for compensation for risk-taking depends on their perception of the risk to their investment, and the number of investors willing to supply capital. This can create market distortions in which, at times, different forms of financing can appear relatively cheap.
7. This is the basis for valuing liabilities in a manner consistent with how the financial markets would value similar instruments, rather than on a 'best estimate' basis. Effectively, market consistency means assessing the price of the insurance for positions exposed to market risks. This insurance is provided through acquiring assets that match the liabilities, and hedging instruments such as put options, for example.
8. Some companies go further and use the term 'capital' to relate to resources raised from capital markets and use other terminology for 'capital management'.

4 Performance Measurement

1. This includes other creditors such as banks.
2. CDOs are a type of structured asset-backed security (ABS) made up of multiple 'tranches' and collateralised using debt obligations such as bonds and loans. The tranches divide up levels of 'security', with 'senior' tranches being less risky than others. As the degree of risk changes between tranches, the level of compensation, either through acquisition price or interest payments, changes to reflect the security of the investment.
3. Since the financial crisis to the end of 2013, in the United Kingdom no company has acquired a business by paying anything for the potential future new business aspect. This may be a reflection of current market conditions, credibility and trust in the assumptions being used to assess 'value', a lack of potential buyers, businesses being traded out of necessity and the buyer having greater flexibility to achieve a good value for the business, the acquirer not being interested in, or seeing additional value for the combined business in the new business generating capability of the acquisition, aiming instead for cost synergy, or the acquisition being in distress such that its new business generating capabilities are near zero anyway.
4. Naturally, being part of managing a business day to day will bring with it greater contact with information about the business than will be available to external stakeholders who review the business performance, say, quarterly. The 'transparency with which the organisation is run' is about reducing the actual and perceived information asymmetry that exists between internal staff and external stakeholders.
5. That is, enhance return but take less risk.
6. This is a driver for a secondary measure to understand the velocity of capital analogous to the velocity of cash measure mentioned previously.
7. It should be noted that for many general insurance and recurrent premium products, the RARLEC assessment might be performed, allowing for the likelihood of policy renewals if this is a better reflection of business economics. Thus, the timing of the capital requirements associated with the renewed policies will need to be considered as well.
8. Franchise value is defined as the present value of a company's prospective *new* investments. Therefore, it is possible to argue that this dimension should be called the enterprise value dimension, as brand and reputational damage can impact the future profits from in force business as well as new business. For example, brand damage could cause existing customers to lapse or surrender their policies, thus reducing the value of future profits from in-force business.
9. The regulator is concerned with ensuring that a company has sufficient capital to
   a) pay salaries to manage the business while it is in existence
   b) buy the insurance or reinsurance to mitigate the risks associated with meeting all the promises the business has made to date, and
   c) hold a buffer sufficient for the business to withstand a material adverse event and still have sufficient funds in order to initiate and deliver a controlled winding down of the business. The regulatory balance sheet is more focussed

on ensuring the company's ability to deliver for existing customers than making an allowance for future levels of new business growth.

10. Under Solvency 2, this links closely with the demands from Pillar 2 and the own risk and solvency assessment (ORSA) requirements.

11. The size of the economic capital buffer is usual expressed as an amount after allowing for the benefit of diversification. Hence, those organisations with diverse business models, such as composite life and general insurance companies, will have a large amount of benefit from diversification that may mean they appear to have a larger buffer than single-product organisations.

12. Rating agencies may use their own 'balance sheet model' to form the basis of their assessment of the financial strength of the company. Again, this may involve the rating agency making simplifying broad brush assumptions that mean their model infers risk exposures that are not exactly the same as those determined internally for a company's own capital assessment.

13. IFRS is a set of accounting standards that underpin many company accounts. Some companies may still produce their accounts on local accounting regimes that may differ from IFRS.

14. There is an argument that competitors should be monitored as a stakeholder group. In the financial crisis of 2008, when Lehman Brothers collapsed, a statement in the small print of the announcement suggested they were using valuations of assets far higher than other companies. This created some element of panic about the approaches other companies were using and whether the quality of other companies disclosures could also be trusted. This contagion risk may be a reason to monitor the stakeholder group.

5   Stress and Scenario Testing

1. 'Sensitivity testing' is another form of assessing single, or multiple, parameter changes. However, the term is used to refer to small changes rather than extreme changes. This approach is useful if there is sparse data on which assumptions have been set, for which we want to understand the implications for pricing and provisioning of misestimating the basis as a result of incomplete data.

2. This illustrates the added importance of defining the business model discussed before. RST becomes more relevant, valuable and insightful, the better the articulation of the business model.

6   Operationalising the Management of Solvency and Capital

1. The green zone is the target zone in which the Board is comfortable. The amber zone is the position in which the Board would like to understand what actions management is planning and how it believes the business will return to the green zone. The red zone is where the Board does not want to be and at which it expects actions to be taken should the position reach these levels.

2. The 115 per cent represents the target solvency ratio for the legal entity that has been agreed upon with the Group, which is higher than the local regulatory

requirement of 100 per cent. The reason for the difference is explained later within this section.

3. Breaching regulatory capital requirements does not mean that the company is technically insolvent, as it has capital in excess of what is expected to be required to meet obligations to policyholders.

4. 'Unmodelled management action' is a phrase that refers to management actions that have not been embedded within the models that are used to calculate the reported solvency position. Thus, these are actions that can improve the solvency position from that reported previously.

5. The operational buffer is not the same as the target economic capital requirement.

6. International Financial Reporting Standards (IFRS) loss-making entities may not be able to pay dividends, therefore resulting in trapped capital.

7. The book continues to use the term 'business unit' and does not adopt a different terminology associated with a management structure in the explanations that follow.

8. As a result of business performance, opportunities exist for the budget to be re-allocated and new limits set. Generally, this would be part of the reforecasting process in which underperforming units might have their budget re-allocated to units that provide propositions to utilise the capital and enhance return. It is not that these budgets are fixed at the start of the year and opportunity does not exist for them to be reassessed.For a Group, fixing the capital budget also means that the value of diversification for which a business unit can take credit in its pricing and risk management needs to be fixed so that the fortunes of one business unit are not impacted, favourably or otherwise, by the performance of another business unit.

7   Risk and Capital Modelling

1. For example, certain forms of financing from capital markets is restricted in its use to cover the buffer capital that is required.

2. This is referred to as a market consistent approach.

3. These interest rates are applicable to new business policies written in the period and fixed for the remainder of the term of the policy (i.e. interest rates for in-force business are not reviewed at each subsequent valuation, new interest rates are only determined for the latest new business).

4. The experience may include claims payment patterns, policy surrender or lapse rates, or policy option take-up rates.

8   Structuring the Use of Risk Information

1. Regulatory definitions of operational risks specifically exclude strategy risk and losses arising from events that give rise to reputational damage. This is because the focus of the regulatory balance sheet is less about future new business capability, for which these risks and issues are important. As the primary focus of the risk register is to support the management of the business, these dimensions

should be included and considered in populating the data in the register, but excluded from data analysed to support the regulatory reporting requirements.
2. The benefits can include preventing adverse damage to reputation and brand.
3. The risks may be further classified into categories such as financial market risk, credit counterparty risk, liquidity risk, business and underwriting risks and operational risks.

9   Risk Culture

1. Including legally possible.
2. Simply put, revenue is earned by taking risk, and earning more revenue can be achieved by taking more risk. However, the risk is that things might not turn out as expected and that the business might turn out to be extremely loss making.
3. If external stakeholders become aware of an inconsistency between internal and external communications, there can be a breakdown of trust that can take a long time to rebuild.

10   The Board and the New Chief Risk Officer

1. This may include operational issues such as that the approach to investing has been agreed upon appropriately, which means that the company follows an ethical investment policy.
2. For example, these may include sensitivities to key assumptions such as market share, average policy size and retention rates.
3. This should include an assessment of the effectiveness of a proposed response plan against the speed with which the risk will manifest itself.
4. There is an information asymmetry between what the Board sees and knows, and what is known purely from being embedded within an organisation on a daily basis, seeing all the information and interacting with all employees. To this end, the Board is reliant on the CRO to be able to collate, interpret, question and distil this information on behalf of the Board.

Index

The manufacturer's authorised representative in the EU is Springer
Nature Customer Service Centre GmbH, Europaplatz 3, 69115 Heidelberg,
Germany. If you have any concerns regarding our products, please
contact ProductSafety@springernature.com

Printed and bound by CPI Group (UK) Ltd, Croydon, CR0 4YY
23/04/2026
02095595-0018